Normandy to Nazi Surrender

Firsthand Account of a P-47 Thunderbolt Pilot

D1563898

Colonel Van H. Slayden, USAF

With Patrecia Slayden Hollis

Black Rose Writing | Texas

ISBN: 978-1-68433-623-4
PUBLISHED BY BLACK ROSE WRITING
www.blackrosewriting.com

Printed in the United States of America
Suggested Retail Price (SRP) $16.95

Normandy to Nazi Surrender is printed in Gentium Basic

Cover photo from the Aviation History Online Museum: P-47 Thunderbolt
Fighter-Bombers in formation—the Juggernauts of World War II

*As a planet-friendly publisher, Black Rose Writing does its best to eliminate
unnecessary waste to reduce paper usage and energy costs, while never compromising
the reading experience. As a result, the final word count vs. page count may not meet
common expectations.

For American fighter pilots, including the 20th century pilots who created a legacy for those in the air today. Coming from all parts of our country, the Army Air Corps' early fighter pilots developed and refined the art of flying in combat. Some never made it to war—some never made it back. All were courageous.

Patrecia Slayden Hollis, November 25, 2020

Normandy to Nazi Surrender

Table of Contents

Annexes

Foreword

These memoirs capture the life of an early 1900's country boy, Colonel Phillip Van Hatton Slayden (1913 – 1996), US Air Force (USAF) retired, who grew up in small-town Waverly in rural Tennessee, and fought across Europe in World War II. Like so many of his contemporaries, he stepped up to the challenge as part of the Greatest Generation and helped define America as a superpower.

In 1938 he graduated in Pursuit Aviation at the Army Air Corps' (AAC's) Advanced Flying School, Kelly Field, Texas, as a second lieutenant. He and other early fighter pilots developed and refined the young AAC's (established in 1926) operations, tactics, techniques, and training that served our nation well in World War II.

In June 1944, Van Slayden crossed the English Channel shortly after the invasion of Normandy to help establish a US Army Air Forces' (USAAF's) forward presence in Europe. He flew P-47 Thunderbolt fighter-bombers in Northern France and commanded the 36th Fighter Group—"The Fightin' 36th"— for missions over Belgium and the Rhineland. He was deep into Germany at Brunswick when the US First Army halted at the Elbe River, facing the Russian Allies on the other side. The Nazis officially surrendered on May 8, 1945, a strange day.

Van Slayden was a character, risk taker, and an adventurer. He lived what he believed and, for the most part, had fun doing it.

Patrecia Slayden Hollis

Chapter 1: Army Air Corps Training and My First Assignment

I graduated from Oklahoma City University on May 29, 1936 with a Bachelor of Arts degree. My post-graduate plan was to get on active duty as an officer in the Army. Hitler was making this option easier, and I had Mother's brother, Major George Hatton Weems, a West Point graduate (known as "Uncle Major"), stationed at Fort Sam Houston, Texas, to keep me advised.

In June of 1936, I went on active duty with the 9th Infantry Regiment (2nd Division) at Fort Sam Houston for one year, arranged by Uncle Major. It was an exercise under Congress' Thomason Act to select 1,000 of the best Reserve Officers' Training Corps (ROTC) students to serve for a year in the Regular Army with the top ten percent offered regular commissions at the end of the year. I learned a lot during the exercise: four-year college ROTC graduates came with more training than I picked up in one year of ROTC (and a second year playing the cymbals in the military band for ROTC credit) at the University of Tennessee (UT) in Knoxville, plus two months of Citizens Military Training Camp (CMTC) in the summers. (Because I was a leader in the last CMTC, I had been commissioned a second lieutenant in the Infantry Army Reserve in November 1935.)

At Fort Sam, I experienced an almost McCarthy-like enquiry. The country was terrified of Communism, and college graduates had spent time in academia where everyone thought Communists thrived. I went before a Regular Army Officer Candidate Board, and one of the board members happened to have been an instructor at the ROTC program at the UT during my freshman and sophomore years there. He asked, "Lieutenant Slayden, what part did you play in the Communist Movement at UT in 1932?" I couldn't give him an intelligent answer because I didn't know there was a Communist

Movement at UT. I had been a cartoonist for the *Mugwump*, the UT magazine, and at least one of my cartoons had poked fun at two-year compulsory ROTC. Did that qualify me as part of the Communist Movement? I didn't hear anything more on the subject, but I left the evaluation board with the sure knowledge that I'd never make the cut.

Randolph Airfield was close by, and several lieutenants took the physical exam for Army Air Corps flying training there. So, I took the exam too. To pass the infantry exam, I had received a waiver because my right foot is flat. The Army Air Corps noticed that, but, so what? Pilots fight sitting down. I breezed through everything else and was ordered to report to Randolph Field for pilot training in June 1937, a week or two after my exercise at Fort Sam. Meanwhile, as a high school and college South Paw pitching star, I had found a job pitching professional baseball with the Cloverleafs in Selma, Alabama, part of the Southeastern League. The team was at the top of eight (at that time) levels of minor leagues, in other words, one level below the major leagues.

The job started as soon as I could get there and paid $100 a month. That was a lot more than a cadet flyer's $21 per month but $30 less than a lieutenant made; regardless, I expected a raise the second year after the Cloverleafs saw my pitching.

I summered in Selma as the junior member in a pitching staff of six. I won five, lost five, got in a few good helps and pitched for a lot of batting practices. At the end of the season, the Cloverleafs wanted me to report for the next spring training. But by then, I'd learned a valuable lesson: someone with a college degree is wasting time staying on a team where two high-school dropouts are better—probably always will be better—at pitching than he is. Besides, our monthly $100 was only paid for the months we played.

Army Air Corps Cadet, Class of 1938C. In the waning summer of 1937, I wrote the Air Corps that I had missed the June class for flying training due to my unspecified mishandling of the notice the Air Corps sent me. With luck, the Air Corps replied, "Come in October." I had just enough time to go from Selma for a visit at my hometown, Waverly, a small (population 1,152) rural town in Tennessee, before reporting to Randolph Airfield in Texas.

I became a flying cadet in A Company, J Flight, Primary Flying School, Randolph Field in October 1937. After 17 years of boring classrooms, I found a curriculum I loved because it taught me what I needed to know to fly. Navigation, communications, weather and airplane mechanic classes—I sailed through them, but not meteorology. It was the hardest class in Primary Flying School. Ninety percent of the cadets failed the class, washing many of them out of school and bringing cadets with otherwise good academic records to the brink of washing out with just one more misstep.

I worked hard on meteorology because I knew I wouldn't be half worth shootin' if I failed the Met test. To my relief, I passed with a grade of 79. I also had to push to reach 35 letters per minute in Morse Code on the did-dah machine and then never used it again.

At first, I was a "Dodo." Dodos are the pawns of upperclassmen, but only for three months. Then Dodos became upperclassmen.

I was a "duck in water." God made me to fly, with one exception: my stomach. With the help of a Sigma Nu Fraternity brother flying instructor (who was supposed to wash me out of the training for air sickness and didn't) and an elbow-length, liquid-proof pair of leather flying gloves (that one could fill instead of the airplane), I got over my air sickness and graduated from flying school.

Cadets are supposed to turn in their flying gloves after training. I tried, but the supply sergeant wouldn't accept them. They cost me $4.50, the price of a fun-filled weekend in San Antonio.

The first airplane I flew in training was the PT-3 (Pursuit Trainer). The next was a P-12, a pursuit plane, flown in advanced training. Both were bi-wing, kite-type airplanes without brakes. They landed slowly enough that brakes would be unnecessary extra weight. For proper parking, airmen rushed out, grabbed the wing tips and pushed the planes into position. Those airplanes were the dinosaurs of the day, although the P-12 was a box office attraction, shooting poor old King Kong off the Empire State Building.

Our textbook on airplanes advised that retractable landing gears added 23 percent more weight to the planes and would not be continued on others.

On July 10, 1938, I had my first plane crash. As part of the 61st (Flying) School Squadron in the Advanced Flying School at Kelly Field, Texas (near Randolph Field), I dropped a wing while landing a P-12E and tore the tip of the wing off. It wasn't very serious or even dangerous, but I took a lot of heckling from a buddy who had flown into a fence while landing a couple of weeks earlier. He was paying me back for heckling him.

Toward the end of the course, we had a cross-country flight from Kelly Field to Muskogee, Oklahoma, and back, a 1,000-mile trip, the longest to date. That was a heavy day's work in our little airships.

We had good up-to-date maps of Texas showing the airways marked for night flying. They were made by Rand McNally, and each student pilot bought his for 25 cents.

On October 5, 1938, I, Cadet 6265878, graduated from the US Army's Primary and Advanced Flying Schools, specializing in Pursuit Aviation, at Kelly Airfield as a second lieutenant, *again*—this rank in the Army Air Corps Reserve. (See Annex III for the "Graduates in Pursuit Aviation, A Company, Advanced Flying School, Class of 1938C" on Page 101.)

Langley Field and Andy Gump. My first assignment was at Langley Field in Virginia as a fledgling pilot in the 36th Squadron, 8th Pursuit Group. We were armed with aircraft from P-12s to P-30s. Most of our airplanes were P-30s, called PB-2s. The PB-2 was the only two-seater, single-engine fighter plane to see service. Some misguided aircraft designer added a second seat facing the rear of the PB-2 for an enlisted gunner to defend the airplane's rear while in flight. Just looking at that rear-facing seat made my stomach quiver. Langley didn't have a gunnery range for fighter rear-seat training, so no enlisted man ever rode on my training flights.

The PB-2 was an early version of an airplane with retractable landing gears. A large hand crank dominated the right side of the cockpit. You wanted wheels-up? You cranked them up 49 turns. You wanted wheels-down? You pressed a button and down they came, loudly, gravity taking control. The handles never moved when the wheels came down, but pilots always leaned to the other side of the cockpit, just in case.

Retractable landing gears complicated the art of flying. Little more than a year later, my wheels-up crash landing taught me the truth of the saying, "flying by the seat of your pants."

Then the checklist was born. An inspired crew chief spun off of the funny-paper strip "Andy Gump" and came up with the GUMP checklist. GUMP was the acronym for Gas (on the correct tank), Undercarriage (in the correct position), Mixture (of fuel for the job at hand) and Propeller (set to the correct pitch). That and walking around the plane kicking the tires with a damn good crew chief made the system work.

Shortly before I retired in 1962, I used a half-hour-long checklist before piloting my first jet-age airplane. At that point, I had been "flying a desk" for many years. That checklist never gave me the secure feeling Andy Gump did. My PB-2 crew chief should have received a medal.

The 8th Pursuit Group at Langley was a gung-ho outfit commanded by Colonel William E. Kepner. In those days, the Army (and its Air Corps) required young officers, especially new second lieutenants, to call upon their commanding officers (COs) and ladies with times specified for the couples to receive such calls. Young airplane jockeys fresh out of flight school in 1938 came with hats that stood up stiff, Sam Browne belts, swords, boots (spurs were optional on the ground), and lots of calling cards to leave at the appropriate places in the appropriate numbers when making formal calls on commanders. As one could imagine, a second lieutenant calling on a colonel commanding at the group level was stressful.

Sunday afternoon was an appointed time for such stylized social visits. The rules were that if you called on the commander and no one was at home, then you could push your cards through the mail slot on the front door and receive "credit" for the call.

One Saturday night in the officers' club bar with several flying school classmates, the subject arose that several of us were in arrears for calls on the colonel. It also was discussed that Colonel and Mrs. Kepner were to be out of town the entire weekend, including Sunday afternoon. Because I was unbelievably naive, my peers loaded me down with stacks of cards (three from each lieutenant) to be delivered for credit through the front door of the colonel's quarters the next afternoon.

The time came. I knocked on the door (for the neighbors' sake). I waited (also for the neighbors). I then started shoving handfuls of cards through the mail drop in the colonel's front door...when it opened. Although my mind began to go blank, I do remember my eyes traveled from the colonel's feet to his face as his eyes moved back and forth from my face to the bunch of cards in my hands. I could see the meaning of the situation compute in his eyes. Then, with a broad smile, he asked, "Lieutenant, what are you doing?"

It's hard to remember my response or the details of the conversation that ensued, but there's no doubt about the value of honest confession, especially when the colonel catches you red-handed. I do remember he had me in for a drink; I "called upon" the colonel and his lady for an excruciating 30 minutes. Colonel Kepner had a sense of humor and, while I was at Langley, he never let me forget the incident—especially that I knocked first.

Many years later as a lieutenant colonel, I was going through a receiving line at a formal function in which I was to shake hands with then Lieutenant General Kepner, the Commander of the United States Air Force (USAF), Alaska. (He also had been the CO of the VIII Fighter Command in Europe during the war.) As I stood in line, I thought, "Surely, he won't remember that day I called upon him and Mrs. Kepner...surely *not*." By that time, I had considerably more rank and less hair.

As it came time to shake his hand, I smiled while his aide de camp announced my name. General Kepner hesitated, holding my hand in mid-shake as he stared at my face. Then he burst forth in an enthusiastic smile, pumped my hand, and said, "*Lieutenant* Slayden!"

Flying the PB-2 at Langley had its limitations. Our flights were mostly below 10,000 feet until oxygen was installed. Then above 12,000 feet, pilots bit on the end of a rubber hose, blow-drying our tonsils. That and no heat in the cockpit made flying at high altitudes rare.

The first year I took off with a loaded gun was 1939—two years after I started flying.

Second Lieutenant for the Third (and Last) Time. After a few months at Langley, the PB-2s disappeared, and we were equipped with brand new P-36 Hawks, real joy buggies. We could fly up to 20,000 feet. But the Air Corps was running out of money, so we could only fly four hours per month for most of the same year the war in Europe started.

As it turned out, I put that extra time to good use. The war scare had grown, and so had the Air Corps. Competition for Regular Army slots was fierce. Several hundred Army Reserve lieutenants, such as myself, were to be given an exam with only the top hundred or so getting Regular Army Commissions.

The 8th Group went all out to help its junior birdmen get ready for the exam, and that worked for me. I had plenty of time to study and a set of bachelor quarters in Dodd Hall to myself. Most unfortunately, my roommate from Arkansas, Elton Earl (Gabby) Holcomb, who was a friend and classmate from Advanced Flying School, had been lost over the Atlantic a few weeks earlier.

I papered my quarters with posters of information I needed to know to pass the test—literally all over the walls, ceilings and some of the floor. Navigation was in the bedroom, mechanics in the living room, communications in the kitchen, and weather in the bathroom. I read them morning, noon and night. I read the books to the walls and the walls to the books.

When it came time for me to take the exam, I could shut my eyes and read the answers to questions off the appropriate posters in my quarters. I could find enough of the answers papered on my quarters to come out ranked seventh of 80 lieutenants taking the exam at Langley Field.

On August 15, 1939, I was commissioned a second lieutenant for the *third* and last time, this time in the Regular Army with a career in the making.

I never stopped using the posters-on-the-wall technique. Those posters changed abstract thoughts into ideas and allowed me to visualize them by making them a part of my concrete environment. I established posters, or "visual environments," to be the retainers for difficult memory work; I carried 52 empty, numbered environments around in my head. For example, my one is a bun, two is a shoe, three is a tree, and so on. I got good enough at visualizing whatever I had to remember in or around the bun, shoe, tree, etc., that I could hear a list of 52 things (including numbers or abstract concepts) read in sequence in a short time and immediately recite them back accurately.

By the way, 52 as the number of my mental environments wasn't random; it's the number of cards in a deck. I played pretty good poker in my time—including across Europe in World War II. (I sent my military pay stateside to my wife...and most of my poker winnings.) I also could do fantastic card tricks.

Sometime later, when I was a lieutenant colonel stationed at the Pentagon after the war, I earned quite a reputation for my visual environments. It was during another period in which I had time on my hands.

In those days, there was so much combat-experienced rank at the Pentagon that lieutenant colonels "emptied ashtrays."

I became bored, expanded my memory system to several hundred visual environments and "memorized" the Pentagon telephone directory. Now, that is to say, I put "A to AB" in my bun (page one), "AC to AD" in my shoe, and so on until I went through the alphabetical listing of people's telephone numbers. By the listing of letters on each page, I got good enough to tell about where someone's name would fall in which column—that "George Morrison" was in the left column toward the bottom of Page 44."

Before too long, people with Pentagon phone directories in hand randomly walked into my office and, with no preamble or how-do-you-do, asked me where in the directory they could find, for example, Robert Smurdlap's telephone number. I'd tell them. They'd stare at me, test me again, stare at me, and then leave, talking amongst themselves.

I'm certain money changed hands after many of those encounters. There were several gentlemen who visited my office routinely, each with a new sucker in tow. I never told anyone there how I did it.

While stationed at Langley, one flight was of particular interest: I flew the rear ranks of a PB-2 flight up Pennsylvania Avenue in President Franklin Delano Roosevelt's second inaugural parade.

Chapter 2: The Defense of Panama and Early Fighter Operations

By August of 1939, Hitler's sword rattling had reached a crescendo in Europe. Our country reacted by rushing bachelor officer airplane jockeys from different American airfields with their combat planes to the Panama Canal Zone. The US considered the Panama Canal a valuable and vulnerable outpost.

Rush to Defend the Panama Canal Zone. I volunteered to go, piled everything I owned in the middle of my Air Corps rooms in Dodd Hall at Langley, pushed the government's property against the walls, and took off for Panama with little more than a toothbrush. In a flight of P-36 airplanes from Langley, I flew to Brownsville, Texas, where we waited for two days for further orders. I was over Mexico when the war broke out, flying with a gaggle of 26 pilots, mostly in P-36's, scavenged from Langley Field, Barksdale Field, Louisiana, and Selfridge Field, Michigan. We were rushing to be the first line of defense for the Panamanian outpost.

I use the word, "rushing," because that was the plan. Actually, it took us seven days to get through Central America to Panama—the same amount of time it took ocean-going Army transports to ferry down families of military personnel later that year.

The P-36, a short-range fighter with no external gas tank, made a lot of stops for fuel. The airfields were fair-size, mostly level, grass-covered cow pastures. We landed in the direction indicated by the ubiquitous wind socks— usually the only way we knew the field was not just a cow pasture. The first pilot down radioed back helpful hints on how to land, if he had any.

A field near the town of Veracruz, Mexico, was our first stop outside of the US, and it's a good example of the drill required to refuel. Twenty-six aircraft filtered through that field with half staying overnight or longer. Forces behind the scenes kept drums filled with gasoline stored in unused portions of the airfields. These drums had to be rolled to the airplanes, and gasoline had to be pumped into the planes by hand through a chamois cloth in a funnel held in the gas-tank openings.

Now, the main fuel opening in the P-36 is on the airplane's side. We found out immediately that funnels work poorly sideways. For this and other reasons, we needed more hands, more funnels, and more time than anybody planned for. We had one support C-47 cargo plane (Gooney Bird) available to provide refueling equipment for 26 airplanes that soon were scattered the length of Central America.

The airfield/cow pastures normally serviced one Ford Tri-Motor airplane a week, so our mass of fighter aircraft landing in them attracted hordes of sightseers. The Mexican Army came out and kept the crowds from overwhelming us. With all that fuel sitting around and being pumped into planes, fire was a threat. So the Mexican soldiers confiscated our cigarettes. Funny thing, we never got them back.

Language was a problem at Veracruz. Interpreters were limited to one six-year-old son of an American Oil Company employee. The boy understood English and communicated our needs to his Nanny who gave instructions to our Mexican assistants. The communication process left a lot to be desired.

Also, at Veracruz, our drinking water ran out. Our reserve supply was somewhere else in Central America in the Gooney Bird, and drinking local water was not an option. Warm Mexican beer was available in quantities, but I can vouch that two days on that is enough. Guatemala is remembered fondly for its American Embassy with good drinking water and bottles for carry-out to Panama.

We navigated through Central America by looking out the windows of the cockpit and recognizing formations on the ground, right out of geography books. In the clouds, we could fly on "needle, ball, and airspeed" (three separate instruments) but only under stress and duress. The clouds were full of "rocks," and we had left airway beacons and radio ranges behind in the US. On that trip, we lost three airplanes and one pilot along the Pacific Coast of Costa Rica.

At Camp David, Panama, one jump to the Canal Zone, an aircraft starter wouldn't work. P-36 engines were started by placing a 10-gage shotgun shell in a breech and pulling a trigger that kicked the propeller into action. The process worked with disquieting spewing and nerve-racking breech swelling until the propeller turned to relieve the pressure.

At Camp David, we had a defective breech and no spare parts within a thousand miles. Our Gooney Bird brought us what amounted to a big "rubber band"—the backup system. We had heard of the system, but none of us had used it. The crew chief had a book on it; we went strictly by it.

The big rubber band was an elastic rope about 30 feet long with a heavy leather and metal boot on the end to fit over a propeller blade tip. Properly pulled by half dozen men, the rubber band could spin the propeller. The pilot stayed in the cockpit while another pilot straddled the engine in front of the cockpit where he could reach the propeller. The boot was placed over the tip of the propeller blade pointed a few degrees less than straight up. The rope from the boot went forward and down under the propeller hub and off to the pulling crew grouped at one side of the plane. Another rope (regular) was pulled out in front of the aircraft at a right angle to the elastic rope and tied to a parachute harness that I was wearing. With that second rope, it was my job to deflect the heavy boot when it flew free from the propeller as the plane sputtered to life, diverting it away from the crew pulling the elastic rope...and me.

I objected to being tied to that second rope. But the elastic-rope crew was unanimous and adamant—they wanted insurance the boot would be deflected away from them.

The crew pulled hard and stretched its rubber band. The pilot straddling the engine pushed the propeller forward until the elastic rope took over and spun it like a top. The boot whistled harmlessly into the space between the pulling crew and me with all of us tumbling around in the grass. It worked. But, even then, 1,000 miles didn't seem like too long a wait for a spare part.

The last hop to Albrook Field near Panama City on the Pacific side of the Canal Zone was uneventful. After all the hoopla created in assorted Central American airfields, landing at Albrook was anticlimactic—in no way abated by a small group of irate ranking officers who had expected us days earlier. Albrook Field had a long concrete runway, cool clear drinking water, good bachelor officers' quarters, and a functioning officers' club.

We pilots were a fairly normal looking, poorly organized group of individuals from various parts of the states with diverse backgrounds, training and opinions on what ought to be done next. We were part of the 24th Pursuit Squadron (Interceptor) in the 16th Pursuit Group (Interceptor) with the mission of defending the Panama Canal—developing tactics, techniques, procedures, and training to support the mission.

As the defense of Panama grew, the 24th Squadron provided the commanders of new squadrons for the 16th and 32nd Fighter Groups. A remarkable number of us went on to command fighter groups, wings and higher level units during World War II. The air operations we developed to protect the Panama Canal Zone must have prepared us for combat; 29% of our pilots rose to general officer ranks during and after the war. (See Annex IV – The Making of World War II Warriors: Fighter Pilots in the 24th Pursuit Squadron, 16th Pursuit Group, Albrook Field, Panama on Page 104.)

Three of my friends from the 24th Squadron who flew down Central America to Panama with me in mid-1939 faced unique and dangerous challenges during the war—one was fatal.

Eugene Louis Clark from Selfridge Field was the deputy CO of the 352nd Fighter Group (P-51 Mustangs) in the European Theater when he was shot down. He was a German prisoner of war from May 1944 to April 1945—most of the war.

R.R. Rowland, also from Selfridge, commanded the 348th Fighter Group (P-47 Thunderbolts) from November 1943 to June 1945 in the Pacific Theater. He became a Fighter Ace with eight confirmed enemy aircraft kills and retired as a major general.

Clarence Leonard (Bud) Tinker Jr. flew down from Barksdale. Major General Clarence L. Tinker, an Osage Indian born in Indian Territory (Oklahoma), was Bud's father. While Bud Tinker was still in Panama, his father, the CO of the Seventh Air Force in Hawaii, selected himself as flight leader of a dangerous B-24A Liberator bombing mission over Wake Island in the Battle of Midway on June 7, 1942 and crashed into the ocean. He was the first American general officer to die in action during World War II. The Oklahoma City Air Depot was renamed Tinker Field after General Tinker. Today, Tinker Air Force Base is the largest of the Air Force Materiel Command's three Air Logistics Centers.

In March 1943, Major Bud Tinker's last assignment was as the Operations Officer for the 14th Fighter Group (P-38 Lightnings) based in North Africa. While leading a flight of P-38's out of Tunisia toward Italy on May 18, Bud left the cover of a cloud bank and boldly confronted a superior force of German fighters. Bud Tinker crashed into the Mediterranean Ocean. Like his father before him, Bud died at sea.

Parachuting into the Pacific Ocean. Flying pursuit planes in Panama was hairy business. For example, in route to Rio Hato Gunnery Range for training on November 1, 1939 during the rainy season, I had to parachute into the Pacific Ocean in waters known to have sharks.

I was in the Number Two wing position of the third element of a nine-ship flight of P-36A's in a V formation. We observed a squall ahead at Chame Pass in the Chame Mountains. From 2,000 feet and 10 miles away, it was a totally unimpressive small shower line in an otherwise sunny day.

Our flight leader was deceived and chose to drop down and visually follow the white surf of the Pacific Coast line near the Chame Mountains. He flew at approximately 500 feet off the water with the flight echeloned up and out over the ocean. The Chame Mountains were on my right. Presumably, the leader lost his bearings with the rain hitting his windshield and turned sharply out to sea and then down into the ocean.

I was under the impression that the entire formation was in a steep diving turn. Then I saw a flash of fire and foam when the leader's aircraft hit the water but was unable to distinguish the surface of the water or the airplane in the squall. I attempted to level my plane and then gain altitude. I knew the flight formation below me had disintegrated, and seven pilots were shooting up from the ocean and away from the mountains, trying to avoid other airplanes as they flew out of the squall. I was blinded by the rain from all directions and my flight instruments were swinging so violently that I couldn't get coordinates from them. So I pointed my airplane up. As I climbed, my altimeter was above 1,000 the last time I looked at it.

At 110 miles per hour (MPH) airspeed, I lost control of the plane and felt the shuddering effects of the engine stalling. I rolled my canopy back and slid out of the left side of the cockpit by kicking away with my feet; the tail of the plane bruised my shoulder before I could get clear. A short time after my parachute opened, I saw the flash of fire and foam of my plane striking the water below and slightly to the right of my position. I heard my engine motor stop. Strangely, I hadn't noticed the engine sound until it stopped.

The parachute had snapped me up, and I felt like I was hanging still without movement in a world that was quiet in dull shades of gray. Up was where my parachute was, down was where my feet were dangling. When the dull gray changed, my entire world changed quickly.

Suddenly I could see the white caps of the ocean's surface. I slipped out of the parachute just before striking the water and inflated my Mae West life vest as I hit the waves. I stayed with the parachute that floated in the ocean with air pockets under it for about 15 minutes until the storm began to dissipate. The parachute gave me a false sense of security—protection from any sharks that might come around. Finally, I could see Chame Pass about three miles away.

I cut the jungle kit loose from my parachute seat that was a flotation device and tied the kit to my Mae West. I used the small machete in the kit to cut my pants legs and shirt sleeves off so I could swim faster. I then tied the machete to my wrist, making it handy for any sharks that might come calling. The thought of spending the night in the ocean with sharks inspired me to swim for shore. To my relief, I never saw a shark.

I swam for about 45 minutes until the OA-9 amphibious plane from Albrook Field rescued me. I never saw any of the other pilots or airplanes in my flight formation. I later learned that the pilot of the plane immediately below me that I guided on had ridden out of the storm clouds trying to pull a cranky canopy loose to bail out.

Of course, our flight leader was killed. We lost planes and pilots off and on in the 24th Squadron, including two experienced first lieutenants sent to lead squadron flights. We expected such losses and didn't dwell on them or we'd lose our focus on the mission and confidence to execute it. We fighter pilots had egos—and they served us well. The next day, we completed the flight to Rio Hato for training in good shape.

Months later, I received a letter from the Irvin Air Chute Company, Inc., in Buffalo, New York, dated May 27, 1940. It said, "Be advised...we have added your name to our list of Caterpillar Club members, and we also have had the official insignia of the club [a caterpillar pin] engraved with your name and the date of your jump. We are enclosing [it] herewith....We trust that you may never again be forced to make an emergency jump, but if you should and are equipped with an Irvin, you may depend on it to bring you safely to earth."

Two More Crashes. On December 7, 1939, I crashed a P-36A in takeoff at Albrook Field. I taxied my airplane out on the runway and tried to take off with an empty tank of gas. With two gas tanks on the plane, I picked the one without gas.

Before I started, I looked at the gas gauge and misread it. Both the full and zero markings were side-by-side on the circular face of the instrument, and I was in a hurry to get out to a firing range where a tow-target plane was waiting for me.

I had enough gas to lift off the runway five feet before the fuel warning light flashed and the motor quit. I tried to reach across to the gas line valve to switch to the other tank but knocked off one of the landing wheels against the runway.

From then on, I concentrated on stopping the airplane. With two or three more good bounces, I tried to beat the other wheel off so the aircraft would slide to a stop on the runway—but it ran off the runway before I could do it.

Next I tried to ground-loop the plane by digging in one wing, but I was going too fast. All it did was dig out a chunk of ground, and sling the plane forward.

When I realized the plane had slowed a bit, I picked out a soft-looking spot on the side of a hill directly in front of me and sailed into it. After my head banged against the side of the cockpit, I cut the switches and jumped out. I nearly broke my neck running to a safe distance from the aircraft with my parachute strapped on behind me dragging through a mess of tall weeds and brush. The airplane didn't catch fire.

Most crashes at Albrook just messed up a wing tip or fouled up a landing gear. But I totaled that P-36.

I was having a bad couple of months. On January 29, 1940, I crashed a P-36A in the corner of a field at Jauqui, Panama, near South America. I was in a flight of P-36's on a routine cross-country mission trying to land in one of those pasture fields we used in the boondocks. Both landing gears came down, but the right one folded back up into the wing when I started to land. I had to make a sort of one-wheel, one-wing-tip landing, which turned out very well for me but completely used up the airplane. I exited the plane rapidly because I had slammed into a large anthill while landing. Beside the ant bites, the worst I suffered was sunburn when I had to wait several hours for a two-seater airplane to come get me.

Other P-36 pilots in the flight witnessed this crash, including my CO, who gave me credit for handling the equipment malfunction well. But the wisecracks still abounded: "It's a good thing Lieutenant Slayden was the pilot who had the malfunction because he has become an expert at crashing." Or, "Lieutenant Slayden is now an 'Enemy Ace' for 'bringing down' three US airplanes." Another, "Albrook Field has just enough airplanes for Lieutenant Slayden's two-year tour in Panama—that is if no one else crashes an airplane."

Wisecracks and heckling each other about flying mistakes, some mechanical and not the pilot's fault, but some the pilot's fault, were coping mechanisms, ways for everyone to get past the incidents. Humor was added to gloss over the potential for injuries or deaths we faced in routine operations. Silence after a serious incident would have been worse.

This period of my "loose use" of government equipment did not go unnoticed by the front office. A personnel shortage existed, and I had the opportunity to fill in as Transportation Officer, Water Rescue Officer, and Provost Marshal.

Once during political unrest in Panama City, I set up a defensive line to protect our ammunition dump, including staking out fields of night fire for two machinegun positions in accordance with infantry instructions received at Fort Sam Houston. A Panamanian civilian got wounded sneaking around the dump one night, but not seriously. That and pitching for the Air Corps' Team in the Canal Zone Baseball Championship (and winning) helped return me to front-office favor and full-time flying.

We had problems with the P-36. Accidents occurred without apparent cause. Rumors surfaced about pilots having strokes, fainting, overheating in cockpits not designed for the tropics, and being mesmerized by instruments. Major Arthur Bump, our commander, put in writing an order he was instructed to give us verbally—"No aircraft is to dive steeper than 35 degrees." The idea that US fighters defending the Panama Canal could not dive steeply enough to defend the canal was not one for publication. Heads rolled. Unfortunately, one of those heads was Major Bump's.

Then two pilots in separate planes landed one day feeling poorly. They were rushed to the hospital, and carbon monoxide was found in their blood. Hairline cracks in exhaust collector rings were located. That and talk about boundary layer airflow patterns led to our improving the P-36's maintenance and the health of our pilots immediately.

It was 1940, and the British in the Battle of Britain were changing the nature of air warfare with the very high frequency (VHF) radio that increased range and ground control of aircraft in the air and, soon, radar. In Panama, our radios had a range of only 35 miles, and radar was not yet a word in our vocabulary. (The first radar control system was introduced in Panama in late 1941, but I had transferred back to the states before the system came on line.)

We maintained proficiency by flying at night on instruments, simulating dogfights, patrolling the canal, and practicing gunnery at Rio Hato. We also flew lots of show-the-flag missions all over Central America and, when we got the new P-40 Warhawk fighters with bigger fuel tanks, as far south as the island of Trinidad off the coast of Venezuela.

We fretted about how to attack ground targets. With two .30-caliber machineguns on each P-36, we used a Civil-War-style aerial close-order drill to get a six-airplane flight on the target at the same time for maximum firepower. We hoped to surprise the enemy and limit his ground fire's ability to concentrate on each plane. When we were issued P-40s in 1941 with eight .50-caliber guns on each airplane, close-order drill in air combat was left to the bombers.

Artificial horizons for instrument flying became much improved about this time. We had been dependent on needle, ball, and airspeed to fly in clouds because earlier artificial horizons models had a disturbing tendency to "tumble" and become useless when the airplane went into a turn or rough weather. With improved models, instrument flying came of age.

Chapter 3: Army Life and Founding the Home of Fighter Pilots

Along with all this flying, I had a love life, starting in 1939 with Mary Caroline Ellis. A few weeks after I landed in the Canal Zone, my personal effects arrived from Langley Field, including my car. I dressed up in a new US Army Air Corps white uniform made for social activities in the tropics, and the time came for me to broaden my horizons. I went cruising that evening and spotted 18-year-old Caroline at a social gathering with a mutual friend. I moved in for an introduction. I found myself dancing with the friendliest, prettiest girl I had ever met. She was the daughter of Lieutenant Colonel Daniel M. Ellis, second in command of the 5th Infantry Regiment, a unit new in the Canal Zone digging itself a base in the nearby jungle.

Caroline and the Army Air Corps. Caroline Ellis was a "Panamanian Princess," one of five finalists in the Panama Canal Zone beauty contest—a well-deserved royal title.

Dancing with her was fun, so I made a date with her for a Tuesday in two weeks' time, the earliest I could get a date. Others had booked her up.

Human frailties being what they are, I blew that perfect beginning. Come Wednesday two weeks, I had missed that date. I plain forgot. Immediately, I wrote a reasonably vague note of apology and dispatched it with a box of candy. Her reply came whistling back: "Unsatisfactory! A proper explanation would be better than six boxes of candy!" I bought five more boxes of candy, and delivered them with as much charm as I could muster.

Although Caroline was still miffed with me, her father got a big laugh out of it and suggested she accept another date with me so I could come over and eat the cheap candy I had bought.

Our social activity in the Canal Zone revolved around the officers' club. Albrook Field's club was a poor place to bring a new girlfriend. It was polluted with 20 to 30 bachelor lieutenants fresh from the states. Given the scarcity of appropriate places to go in the evenings at the Canal Zone, I had no choice but to take her to the Saturday evening dances. Thereafter, my social life with Caroline had to conform to the impact of surplus suitors.

Finally, I had, had enough dates with her to convince her she loved me and that we should get married. Maybe it was because I was more impressive as a new first lieutenant and the new CO of the 29th Fighter Squadron, 16th Fighter Group. Or maybe not. A lieutenant is a lieutenant except when that rank precedes colonel or general.

I received permission from Colonel Ellis to marry his daughter, and I wasn't waiting around for anyone to change his or her mind: Caroline and I were to be married in two weeks.

It just so happened that the 1941 Canal Zone Baseball Championship was about to be played. Colonel Ellis was very proud of his 5th Infantry Team. So as time and banter would have it, a bet ensued. He bet that if his team won, I would pay all the expenses of the wedding; if his team lost, he would pay the groom's wedding expenses as well as his own. I pitched and my team won. I married Mary Caroline Ellis on April 26, 1941 at Albrook Field in the Canal Zone at the Episcopal Church, Saint Luke's Cathedral, all expenses paid.

Much to her chagrin, I often claimed that I won Caroline in a baseball game, which is not entirely true, of course...but pretty close.

Of interest, after being married for a couple of months, I learned Colonel Dan Ellis' history. As a young man, he walked out of a dirt floor cabin and down the mountains of east Tennessee one day and joined the Army as a horse holder. He fought in World War I, and then retired as a lieutenant colonel in the Army in 1943. He could play a "mean" fiddle and preferred goat's cheese. I always called him "Colonel" (never in later years, "Dan") out of absolute respect for him.

About the time Caroline and I got married, Panama got the attention of our nervous headquarters, and P-40 fighter aircraft were assigned to defend the Canal Zone. These were the first new combat airplanes in the US. My 29th

Squadron was scheduled to be one of the first to get the P-40s, so I was ordered to pick up a flight of nine new P-40Es in Ohio and bring them to Panama. As it later turned out, my nine P-40s were rated combat ready and placed on "General Alert" on December 7, 1941—the infamous day the Japanese attacked Pearl Harbor.

The assignment to lead P-40s from Ohio to Panama was of such magnitude that it prevailed over plans for a honeymoon. That, as I discovered, is a poor way to start a life of matrimony. It was a long-term blessing that I married an Army Brat and was not the one who introduced her to our lifestyle.

Buzzing My Hometown. I picked up a flight of P-40s from Wright Airfield near Dayton, Ohio, checked out in the aircraft, and led them back to Panama. This trip through Central America would stay on schedule, taking a matter of hours—it was a far cry from our trip two years earlier flying P-36's. But it just so happened that my hometown Waverly was directly below one leg of that flight plan, and I was flying the newest, hottest fighter airplane in service.

The situation overwhelmed me. I put Number Two Bird Boy in charge of the flight and went down for a "tree-top reconnaissance" of Waverly. I was an experienced fighter pilot with 500 flight hours, still alive, and on my first trip home. I buzzed Waverly at 250 miles per hour and left Waverly's streets full of people (the population had risen to 1,318 in 1940), staring up at the sky as the tree tops thrashed and whipped from my P-40. That was fifty-odd years ago; occasional comments about that visit still surface from mature Waverly natives.

At the time of our marriage, we were planning a honeymoon trip to Haiti to visit now Colonel George Hatton Weems, who was Chief of the US Military Mission to Haiti. Uncle Colonel had large quarters, a cook and servants. Instead, we took the "standard" Pacific-side honeymoon trip, going by train to the Atlantic side and spending three days in a hotel—*after* I picked up the P-40s in Ohio. The trip was far from the fun Caroline anticipated that a trip to Haiti would have been.

Lindy Ellis and Me. A short time later, Colonel Ellis was transferred back to the states and, in addition to his daughter, he left his dog, Lindy, with his lieutenant son-in-law to bring when I transferred stateside in a few months. Dogs were not allowed on family transport boats back to the states. Caroline warned me that Lindy was a very important person (VIP) in the Ellis family. When I received orders for Luke Airfield, Arizona, in October 1941, special procedures were required to handle Lindy. I tied him to a post at our then emptied quarters and put Caroline aboard a military transport boat on the Pacific side of the Canal headed for the Atlantic side. The transport still didn't allow dogs.

I picked up Lindy at the apartment and stuffed him into a GI bag. With my good friend Lieutenant Clint Wasem, we checked out an A-10 airplane, and with Lindy on my lap in an open cockpit two-seater aircraft, we flew across the Isthmus of Panama to France Field on the Atlantic side of the canal. I could tell Lindy approved of me letting his head out of the bag after we were airborne, but that clearly was the last pleasant thought he had about me or anything else until we were back on the ground.

The newly appointed CO of France Field was Major Arthur Bump, late of Albrook Field. We had a party. It was restrained because Wasem and the airplane had to return to Albrook Field the next day in good order.

The next morning, Lindy boarded the banana boat and I joined Caroline on the Army boat for our trip back to the states. Caroline was pregnant and sick every hour of everyday of the week on that boat. When we got to New Orleans, we unexpectedly had to wait three days for Lindy's banana boat to come in. That probably was Lindy's doing.

We visited Colonel Ellis for a short spell in Denver, Colorado, and then traveled on to Luke Field near Phoenix for my new station. The truth be told, I knew Lindy was not Number One on the Colonel's list—but he outranked me.

War in Southern California. Luke Field was an airfield under construction to train fighter pilots and, in the years to come, gained the reputation as the Home of Army Air Corps Fighter Pilots. We had to work out of tents on the edge of a very large concrete landing mat in between areas still under construction. We received student pilots from other schools; topped them off with two months' finishing school in the AT-6 aircraft, an advanced trainer, commissioned them as second lieutenants, and passed them on to specialized aircraft and mission training.

The Japanese attack on Pearl Harbor, December 7, 1941, just a few weeks after we arrived in Arizona, immediately caused a great deal of confusion. There was concern that the invasion of the West Coast might be eminent. Along with a number of other pilots from other airfields who had varying degrees of experience, I rushed west to March Airfield, California, to defend our nation (Special Orders No. 158). It was an exercise so much like the rush to defend Panama that it was scary. But this time, we didn't take airplanes.

Colonel Ellis came to Luke Field, gathered up his pregnant baby daughter, and took her back to Denver.

An endless stream of rumors surfaced about California: "The Japanese were shelling the coastal areas as a prelude to invasion" or "Japanese Americans were forming militias in the back country." Blackout was proclaimed for the entire area, but it had little effect because people were allowed to use car lights to get to and from wherever they were going to be "blacked out."

I was billeted with Major Robert L. Scott, later renowned for his book *God is My Co-Pilot* that he wrote about his experiences in China. I was the closest thing to a co-pilot he had in California.

We, a disorganized mass of individuals, eager to defend our nation, descended upon the March Airfield operations officer. We learned startling facts: no one was expecting us, and we had no airplanes to fly, no organization to report to, and nothing to do—except to stay the hell out of other people's way. After all, they had a war to fight.

Later, in the officers' club bar, we organized an unidentified unit with Major Scott, commanding, and Lieutenant Slayden, Adjutant. I collected a list of 20 or 30 of our names, long since lost. We located a hangar with P-40s down for maintenance, and we gave fellow pilots not checked out in that new combat aircraft cockpit-familiarity sessions. That was the sum total of our contribution to the War in Southern California.

We hung around the officers' club bar for two weeks and were ordered back to our home bases. So much for my second dash forward to defend my country.

But it could have been worse. Major General Herbert Dargue, my former CO in Panama, died December 12 in an airplane crash in the Sierra Nevada Mountains with several of his staff officers. They were in route from Washington, DC, to Hawaii via California. I could have been part of his staff.

Defense of Arizona and Training Fighter Pilots. Back at Luke Field, our war effort stepped up to a seven-day week, but until the student supply system cranked out more trainees, we hunted for work. I got leave to bring Caroline back from Denver and set up housekeeping again.

For weeks after returning from California, I was assigned the mission of defending Arizona on orders from Washington. (I qualified for the mission by not yet being embedded in the training structure.) The orders implied the probability that the Japanese would land in southern California and launch an attack on Washington, DC, through Arizona. Washington recognized we were not equipped or prepared to defend under such combat conditions but expected that every little bit would help.

We certainly had that "little bit" for Washington. The defend order was vague and our ability minimal. With six AT-6 trainers (two .30-caliber machineguns each), we could cover the aerial approaches to western Arizona. After several futile efforts to devise a plan, we settled on the one feasible one: warn Washington of the Japanese invasion, assuming, of course, that Washington had not already heard California had fallen.

Flying back and forth repetitively across a six-mile stretch of air corridors over the middle of the Arizona desert during daylight hours was not an inspirational activity. However, we did learn that it was quite a thrill, to say the least, if you flew a few feet above the desert floor over the Grand Canyon, which dropped away one mile deep suddenly and then, just as suddenly, closed to a few feet above the desert floor on the other side. I flew that several times as did others, but our commander stopped that practice when one pilot misjudged the other side and plowed his airplane into the far wall of the canyon.

After a spell of patrolling for invading Japanese in Arizona, a farsighted Washington bureaucrat shut such activity down.

Once again, I was tapped to fly a plane to my unit. A request went out for a pilot qualified to fly an A-10 to the East Coast and pick up an AT-6 for Luke Airfield. It just so happened that my two brothers, Lieutenant Al of the Navy and Lieutenant Bill of the Army, were stationed in Washington, DC, and my flight was over Waverly. I had *experience* in an A-10—I had flown across Panama in one with a dog on my lap. I got the mission.

Flying the A-10 from Luke to Albuquerque, New Mexico, was no problem. Aircraft of the 1940's were "birds of a feather," subservient to the GUMP checklist—or almost. In the air over Albuquerque, getting ready to land, I applied the GUMP checklist, but nothing in the cockpit told me the landing gear was down and locked. But nothing said it wasn't. From a pilot's perspective, airplane instruments need to be more positive than that. After all, I already had an emergency landing in Panama and destroyed an airplane because of a landing gear problem.

I called the tower and said I was delaying the landing for a few minutes. I searched that cockpit from canopy to foot pedals. Nothing told me my landing gears were down. I came back to the tower, flew by low and requested a visual check of the gears, which the tower reported "Looked okay." But just in case, the tower alerted fire engines to come to the runway for possible landing problems. I had none.

The rest of the flight was "more positive" because an A-10 crew chief in Albuquerque pointed out a thumb-like gizmo from the wheel well that popped up through a hole in the top of the wing outside the cockpit, verifying for the pilot that the wheels were down and locked.

I had a memorable time with my Navy and Army brothers in DC and was careful to recover from my hangover before flying the AT-6 back to Arizona.

My flight over Waverly? I was now a settled married man about to become a father (and the Air Corps had forbidden buzzing hometowns).

At Luke Field, I commanded a training squadron in the Air Corps' Advanced Flying School for a short time and then became Assistant Director of Training under Lieutenant Colonel Lester S. Harris, Director of Training. We were part of the new 37th Flying Training Wing, also at Luke Field. For almost three years, the Harris-Slayden team squeezed more training into more fighter cadets in less time with each passing month. We daily monitored more than 250 training planes, each with an instructor and student, in the skies over a large section of central Arizona.

The first year, we trained pilots everyday all day and well into the night. We were continually reminded by the powers above that wars don't wait. That was the beginning of Luke Field as the Home of Fighter Pilots in World War II.

Our daughter, Caroline Weems Slayden, nicknamed the "Gremlin," arrived on schedule on March 30, 1942 in Phoenix. I don't remember what the

Gremlin cost, but she was the most expensive of our children. The next three arrived in military hospitals at an average of $12.00 each, and most of that expense was for Caroline's food.

The year 1942 must have been one of chaos in Washington, DC, when they realized they were getting a burgeoning wartime army on hand with not enough people in charge. I was a first lieutenant and "senior" by the time the war started, having been promoted to second lieutenant (the first time) in the Infantry Reserve in 1935. So the Army Air Corps promoted me three ranks in 11 months. I became a captain in February 1942, a major in May 1942, and a lieutenant colonel in January 1943.

In 1943, the shock of war subsided or, possibly, we had become very proficient at outputting trained pilots at Luke Field. Regardless, the stream of flying cadets was reduced and so was our workweek by one day.

In the spare time produced by a six-day workweek, I began looking for gold in the Arizona desert. I received a report that Lieutenant William W. Roberts, one of my flying instructors, was trying to put together time to get married. When his leave request came to me for approval, he also mentioned that his bride-to-be had an uncle who had a map to the legendary Lost Dutchman's Goldmine in the nearby Superstition Mountains. Five days were immediately put together for Robert's wedding—two more than the wartime allotment—with the understanding that he was to bring back a copy of the map along with his bride. He did.

Thus began my and (later) my family's wandering around with me in the Superstition Mountains off and on over decades, looking for the Dutchman's lost stash of gold. (See Annex V - "I am Coronado's Child, Searching for the Lost Dutchman's Goldmine" on Page 107.)

Fort Leavenworth and the Fighting Weemses. After three years of training other pilots for World War II, I attended advanced training before reporting to a fighter group headed for Europe. I was ordered to the Army Command and Staff School at Fort Leavenworth, Kansas, for several weeks to learn how the Army worked. By this time, I was a major and older Brother Bill was a captain and an instructor at the school. Captain Slayden carried Major Slayden's bags into my student apartment.

I was youngest of the three Slayden Brothers in the war effort and the last of the three to enter military service. Oldest brother, Al, an Annapolis graduate, Brother Bill, an Armor officer in the Army, and I were in friendly competition to see who attained rank the fastest. I was winning, at least for the moment.

I also routinely "won" another family competition—the brother who was the baldest. Throughout our adult lives, we three lowered our heads for photographs to document the baldest as the winner...or as in this case, me, the "loser."

In January 1943, Bill, still at Fort Leavenworth, created and served as first editor of *Weemsana*, a family newsletter named after our mother's family (Weems) published four times a year. Its purpose was to maintain contact among the children, spouses and grandchildren of Tennesseans Joseph Burch and Bessie (Rye) Weems serving in the war effort. Joe B. and Bessie were our grandparents. When Bill, then a lieutenant colonel, left for war, Aunt Dockie (Shipp) Weems became the editor for the January 1, 1944 edition. Brother Al, a Navy commander, was already out to sea, location unknown.

Weemsana and the "Fighting Weemses" received national attention from *Time-Life*. An excerpt from *Time* Views the News, Blue Network radio broadcast, November 2, 1944: "And now we are going to take a couple of minutes to tell you about one of the fightingest American families there is. The Weemses of Tennessee. They have so many family members in the armed services that they publish a family newspaper about themselves every couple of months. A nice little tabloid called *Weemsana*. *Time* correspondent William Howland of Atlanta, Georgia, sent us a copy today, and, while we grant you this isn't hot spot news...well anyway, it's good Americana.

"There are 50 members of the Weems family in service. They have top-notchers and buck privates, and there are WAVEs [US Navy's Women Accepted for Volunteer Emergency Services] and WACs [Women's Army Corps]. Among these top-notchers are Brigadier General George Hatton Weems, who is Assistant Commandant of the Infantry School, and over in London, a Major Mary C. Weems has charge of WAC personnel in the London area.

"In Dickson, Tennessee, is a civilian, Mrs. Dockie Weems, who edits this novel newspaper all devoted to the doings of one highly military family....The family paper seldom refers to anybody by the last name—it is always 'Mary

Kate' or 'Susie Ann' or something like that. As correspondent Howland said, 'The paper is as homey as the aroma of frying sausage from a Weems' kitchen in Tennessee.'

"Back in the days of 1861 or thereabouts, Joseph Burch Weems of Tennessee joined the scouts of General Nathan Bedford Forrest. General Forrest was the one who said, 'Get there fustest with the mostest.' Well, ever since, whenever there is a war, the Weemses try to 'Get there the fustest with the mostest.'"

It is of note that *Weemsana* is still being published [2020] but only once a year. It is the official magazine of the Weems Educational Fund, headquartered in Waverly, that was established on January 1, 1939 and endowed by the estate of my bachelor Uncle General, George Hatton Weems, at his death in 1957. The Fund provides college scholarships for "needy, worthy, and deserving students" and for other educational projects, primarily in the three Tennessee counties from which Joe B. and Bessie Weems hailed.

I went from the school at Fort Leavenworth to Georgia for a couple of months of upgraded combat training with the 59th Fighter Group to help prepare me for war.

I had orders to the 48th Fighter-Bomber Group at Walterboro Army Airfield, South Carolina, a unit headed for World War II. To prepare for deployment, I received a memo from the Walterboro CO, dated January 27, 1944, a "Checklist for Individual Replacements for Overseas Movement"—a list of clothing, equipment and documents, both personal and issue, required for combat deployment (see Annex VI on Page 114). At the 48th Fighter-Bomber Group, I was second in command under Lieutenant Colonel Dixon M. Allison.

Caroline (with Child Number Two, more or less halfway ready to be born) and I farmed out the Gremlin (almost two year's old) with my retired in-laws in Avon Park, Florida, and moved to Walterboro Airfield. We lived a soldier's camp-follower's life in a new-fangled "motel" in South Carolina for weeks until I departed for Europe.

At Walterboro, the 48th trained initially on the P-39 Airacobra fighter. It was a special plane, but not in ways pilots had in mind. The engine had been moved to the rear of the cockpit, and a long crankshaft led to the propeller up front. This allowed a 37-mm cannon to be installed and fired through the hub of the propeller. However, the long crankshaft made thumping noises, and the engine weight shifted to the rear created instability. At times, the plane sort of "grabbed the bit in its teeth." No one complained when thousands were sent to Russia in Lend Lease, even though slightly improved.

One upgraded fighter airplane we had in South Carolina was the P-63 Kingcobra. Among other improvements, it took the "P" out of GUMP by automatically controlling the propeller machinery.

Fiery Crash—Fifth and Final. I flew the P-63 one unusually warm winter day at the end of January on a high-altitude training mission, which was not bad now that my tonsils were protected by an oxygen mask. But at 15,000 feet, my propeller started revving erratically. The noise rapidly increased until suddenly there was a loud thump, and the propeller stopped. Smoke was in the cockpit.

I adjusted for fire hazard, picked out a suitable field in which to land, circled to a proper altitude, and made a right-angle turn into a landing approach—in this case, wheels up because South Carolina in the warm weather had become a muddy mess. Then the fire in back burned through the firewall into my cockpit. I changed my procedures and headed directly toward the ground, arriving too fast to land but leaving enough speed to bounce up over a grove of trees at the end of the field. I drove that airplane into the next field as if I were shooting an arrow. That's not in the books, but it worked fine in the South Carolina mud. I slid to a stop.

To exit the P-63 you had to open a door—it didn't have a canopy. Above the door was a big yellow lever marked "Emergency" that you pulled to shove the entire door out of the way quickly. I pulled and shoved. Nothing happened. With fire licking the back of my neck, I reared back and charged the door with all my strength, knocking it away from the aircraft and throwing myself out of the cockpit and across the wing to skid headfirst into the muddy field. In the process, I ground dirt into my burned wrists. My wrists between the uniform sleeves and flying gloves had fourth degree burns as well as the back of my neck between my uniform and leather helmet.

Belly landing a burning fighter plane into a crop field in rural South Carolina in 1944 quickly drew a crowd. One kind lady brought a big dish of home-churned, unsalted butter from the nearest farmhouse and smeared it on my burned places to try to calm the pain. I asked the first driver I saw to take me to Walterboro Field's hospital. He was a feed and seed salesmen making his rounds. He stopped twice to tell people who I was, what just happened, and that he was taking me to the hospital. I politely requested he just drive straight to the hospital.

When we arrived, the Walterboro Emergency Room was on high alert. One of their senior pilots had gone down somewhere and was missing. A glance from a medic at my burned flight suit smeared in mud, blood, and butter, and the next thing I knew I was on my back with needles in me.

Later, the doctor picked out the obvious sticks and rocks in my wrists and decided not to dig around any farther in the wounds. He bandaged over the whole mess. The wounds never became infected.

Over the years, pieces of South Carolina worked their way up near the skin on my wrists, causing unusual lumps—my children found that especially fascinating. On two occasions, doctors split the skin and removed pieces of South Carolina. That must have been good soil because I never had a problem with it.

After two weeks in the hospital, I took Mary Caroline back to Avon Park to stay with my in-laws and the Gremlin for the duration. I then departed for the European Theater with bandages covering tender parts.

Chapter 4: Deploying to Europe and Fighter Wing Operations

I caught up with the 48th Fighter-Bomber Group at Camp Shanks, New York, on February 16, 1944, and we prepared to deploy our three fighter squadrons to war: the 492nd, 493rd and 494th. On March 21, 1944, we left New York on the *Royal Majesty's Service* (RMS) *Queen Mary* headed for an unknown mission in Europe.

The *Queen Mary* was a massive British ship capable of outrunning German submarines. After clearing the harbor, she proved it by sailing "balls out," charging toward Europe —Damn the Submarines! The weather was too cold and raw to be on deck. So I caught up on my sleep in my nice stateroom shared with two other lieutenant colonels. I pulled the bandages off places burned in the crash in South Carolina, taking several scabs with them. It turned out okay, though, because the only water we had to take showers in was salt water.

The highlight of the trip was watching furniture and people bounce around as we roared through a fair-size gale. The weeklong trip was otherwise uneventful.

We arrived in Gourock in the central lowlands of Scotland and rode a train for two days to Royal Air Force (RAF) Ibsley in southern England. The countryside we rode through was beautiful, just like the picture books. I knew I was headed for combat in Europe and didn't speak French or German. But imagine my surprise when I had trouble understanding the British speaking English. It sounded like they didn't use their tongues when they talked.

The 48th was assigned to the Ninth Air Force. (The Ninth Air Force had been reconstituted in the United Kingdom in October 1943 as a tactical outfit to support the battlefield rather than provide strategic bombing.) In April

1944, the 48th Group set up operations in Ringwood, England, using the concrete Beaulie Airfield, 10 miles west of Southampton ("48th Fi Bomber Gp, HQ, APO 9680 c/o N.Y.C., N.Y."). We checked out the pilots on the new P-47 Thunderbolt, a fighter-bomber. That aircraft expanded our combat altitude to 35,000 feet.

A bit about my airpower weapon: the P-47, built by Republic Aviation and introduced in 1942, was a single-seater, single-engine fighter-bomber armed with eight .50-caliber machineguns, four on each wing. It also carried five-inch rockets or up to 2,500 pounds in bombs. A typical load for combat missions was two 500-pound bombs and five-inch rockets. Fully loaded, it weighed eight tons. It was the heaviest and most rugged US fighter in service with armor protecting the pilot. The P-47, a "flying tank," was designed to support high-altitude, short-to-medium-range escort missions as a fighter and be an adept bomber. It was the first piston-powered fighter to fly 500 MPH and the forerunner of today's multirole fighters.

The Thunderbolt had three nicknames in World War II. It was known as the "Jug" for its shape similar to that of a milk jug of the time or, more complimentary, because it was a "Juggernaut" that packed a heavy punch. Some called it the "Warthog" because of its blunt nose like the snout of a pig. Regardless, it earned its place in history as the fighter-bomber workhorse of the Army Air Corps in World War II.

We were in the European Theater. There was a war going on. We had a new combat plane and were highly motivated to train. We flew, flew and then flew some more: dive bombing, glide bombing, convoy patrolling, smoke laying, low-level navigating, and reconnoitering.

Unknown to us at the time, our training was specifically designed to support Operation Overlord, the invasion of France at Normandy that occurred on June 6, 1944. Our first combat mission was April 20 when we flew over occupied France. In May, the 48th Fighter-Bomber Group was re-designated the 48th Fighter Group.

We met no enemy opposition over France as the skies belonged to the Allies. We began attacking ground targets defended by the Germans. At one flight briefing, we were told the Germans were using a lot more tracer ammunition in an effort to make the new pilots in the obvious build-up of Allied airpower nervous. As far as I could tell, it was working.

With combat missions over France, the 48th Group had a lot of new combat-experienced flight commanders, including me. Then I was notified that I was being transferred to the 84th Fighter Wing, a command structure immediately above the 48th and in control of four fighter groups. The reason: to take more responsibility as a lieutenant colonel, my rank. I objected and was informed, considerately, but firmly, that I *was* being transferred. It was something about my having been promoted in the rapidly burgeoning US Army Air Corps to captain, to major, and then to lieutenant colonel from February 1942 to January 1943. I hardly had time to get the brass right on my uniform, much less gain any experience before I was promoted again. A lieutenant colonel at 29 year's old.

Operation Overlord, the Battle of Normandy, was the Allied invasion of German-occupied France. It began with a widespread Allied bombing campaign by 11,000 bombers and fighters just a few hours before the invasion of Normandy on June 6, 1944. German coastal defenses, aircraft production, fuel supplies and airfields were targeted to protect our invading forces. We also bombed communication infrastructure and road and rail links in an attempt to cut off northern France from German reinforcements.

Just before midnight, 1,200 aircraft took off from England with three airborne divisions—the American 82nd and 101st Divisions and British 6th Division—along with glider planes with supplies and ammunition for the paratroopers, headed for drop zones behind German lines. Operation Neptune, the amphibious landings of almost 160,000 Allied forces in more than 5,000 vessels on five beachheads in Normandy, commonly known as D-Day, was executed early the next morning. American forces landed on the beachheads codenamed Utah and Omaha. The most heavily defended and hard fought beachhead of the invasion was Omaha.

Eventually, the Allies committed more than a million troops in the Battle of Normandy.

My former 48th Fighter Group flew P-47's in Operation Overlord. Beginning June 6, the 48th attacked German-held bridges, gun positions, railways, trains, motor transports, and fuel dumps in France plus provided reconnaissance during the Normandy Campaign.

Deployment to France. Before our 84th Fighter Wing sailed across the English Channel into France on June 18, the Army marched us infantry-style three miles to our boat—I suspected to wear us out. Like an army division headquarters (HQ) bringing regiments on line in battle, the 84th Fighter Wing, commanded by Colonel Arthur G. Salisbury, charged across the English Channel into France, 12 days behind the invading ground forces. We were point men in the movement of US Army Air Forces (USAAF) forward to bases in Normandy and Europe.

Disembarking in France, we stepped onto Utah Beach from a pontoon dock and quietly crossed the badly disturbed sand in quick step, ogling the invasion sights. It takes one hell of a lot of stuff to go to war, and that's what we saw. Among the movement, shouting, and war-engine roaring commotion on the beach, there was a group of dismal looking German prisoners in a stockade at our beaching point, silently watching us trudge by in the sand.

As fast as we hit the ground, we were pushed out onto the road, organizing our outfit as we went. We marched several miles to an open field for the night. It was hot, dusty and rough going with vehicles charging through at crossroads, seemingly from all directions. Military policemen (MPs) at every corner kept us going the right way. The scene had the finer points of a damn big maneuver.

French natives, poor looking sorts, stood on various corners and stared at us, occasionally giving us a "V" for victory with their fingers, or working in nearby fields, doing their best to ignore us. It seemed like two or three American soldiers were resting under every bush. Loose numbers of soldiers wandered around, looking like lost tourists.

Finally, we were turned into an open field, much in the manner of cattle. As the Army directed us into the field, we learned our vehicles with our stuff and supplies had gotten lost. It was dark, and no lights were allowed because German aircraft came back at night to bomb the beaches. We stayed up most of the night with a "box seat" view of intermittent World War II fireworks. Then I tried to sleep as antiaircraft guns from several different directions banged away at odd times. It rained.

At daylight, we built a fire, made coffee, and ate cold rations. We saw the muddy field we hunkered in the night before was covered with discarded plops of cosmoline, a goop used to waterproof equipment. It had the characteristics of a meadow muffin without the smell. Later we heard the GI joke going around that the French had improved the common cow.

Four hours after daylight, trucks transported us to the French Chateau la Vivier in central Normandy, the 84th Fighter Wing's first headquarters in France; it was on the main road halfway between St. Mere Eglise on the west and Carentan to the east. The chateau had been the headquarters of a German unit that rapidly abandoned it as Americans landed in France, leaving behind nice furniture and odds and ends of equipment.

It was a major improvement with comfortable, semi-private rooms with first class beds, a formal dining room, and a well-equipped bar. We rigged a hot-and-cold-running shower and set up a movie room. I sometimes dressed for dinner.

Brother Bill and I had visited briefly in London after I found out our group was going to support the invasion of Normandy, but I couldn't talk to him about Operation Overlord because he was new in England and had not been briefed. That was an unnecessary precaution because after I arrived at our 84th Wing Headquarters in Normandy, I learned he already had been in Normandy for four days.

He had invaded Europe with, literally, nothing but permission to fill a slot in the VIII Corps Headquarters' intelligence section. He had managed to acquire a pup tent, sleeping bag and blanket along the way. Bill had slept in his tent in the rain for days when he saw my unit's 84th Wing Headquarters' sign...at the chateau.

A miserable Bill Slayden, badly in need of a shower, clean clothes, and a drink, found me dressed for dinner, drink in hand, and leaning against the chateau's bar. I accommodated his immediate needs and scrounged him equipment, including an air mattress to keep his sleeping bag up out of the mud. My bunkmate Bobby Jones, who later became famous as a golfer, gave Bill his air mattress.

For a very brief period of the war, I helped establish the Air Force's reputation for living a life of luxury well behind the frontlines in between flying brief but hellacious combat missions forward. *C'est la guerre.*

84th Fighter Wing in Normandy. Initially, the 84th Wing was busy coordinating the operational effectiveness of the Ninth Air Force fighter-bomber groups while they moved to new forward bases in Normandy. The first group arrived on June 19, one day after the 84th Wing landed and only 13 days after D-Day.

But that tapered off. The Army had inconveniently invaded Europe at the time its Army Air Forces were transitioning their combat procedures and organization to the war-tested British ground control pattern. The 101st Wing, our companion operational headquarters on nearby Omaha Beach, was reorganized into the IX Tactical Operations Center (TAC) and took control of Normandy air operations.

That left the 84th Wing in the geographic middle of the biggest battle in history, plugging in the incoming phones to the outgoing lines (figuratively speaking) and with time on our hands. We sat up front at ringside and watched the war go on around us.

Later, in November 1944, when the Allies were approaching the German border, the 84th was equipped and reorganized into the XXIX TAC, and we assumed control of up to five Ninth Air Force fighter groups in major airpower campaigns.

Meanwhile, I came under artillery fire. First a friendly unit moved into a nearby field and rattled our old chateau with outgoing rounds. After one especially noisy occasion, an artillery sergeant came to the chateau to check on us. The latest fire wasn't outgoing fire—it was incoming. The Germans were firing back. Obviously, they missed us, but we didn't recognize the difference until the sergeant's visit. After all the Army's ordering me forward to defend Panama, California, and Arizona, I finally was at war in Normandy shortly after the invasion, came under enemy ground fire for the first time, and didn't even know it.

During the 84th Wing's transition, I was occasionally on courier duty. The bridge at Carentan was a bottleneck for courier service between Omaha and Utah Beaches. It was well within German artillery range for a considerable time. Courier and other traffic was controlled and dispatched in organized dashes.

Once an 88-mm shell hit the road in front of us. The five of us American and British officers immediately bailed out of our moving weapons carrier into a ditch. After we remounted, several more shells, spaced about a minute apart, seemed to follow us down the road, each one getting closer. The consensus was they were hunting us specifically—so we raced through the Carentan Bridge at breakneck speed.

At VIII Corps, Bill Slayden, a free thinking, energetic addition to the intelligence section, had carved out his purpose in warfare: maintain on-site surveillance of the corps' Normandy perimeter. For this he was assigned a Jeep and driver, a lieutenant. I joined his reconnoitering jaunts on occasion while things were slow at the 84th Wing.

I especially remember checking on a report that one of the corps' battalions had crossed the Cotentin Peninsula and cut the Germans off at Cherbourg, a fortified city on the English Channel with a deep-water harbor. The objective was to prevent the Germans from reinforcing the city. (The Allies had failed to capture the Cherbourg Harbor, a key objective in the early days of the Normandy Campaign.) Our mission for the corps intelligence section was to reconnoiter the area and, if possible, determine where the German lines in Cherbourg started.

We drove through war-torn St. Mere Eglise. A mile or so to the west, traffic fell off to nothing, and the whole world got progressively lonelier and quieter. We reached the high point of the peninsula leading to Cherbourg, stopped, and gazed over a silent scene that included five freshly killed Germans in a nearby ditch. Obviously there had been a recent fight at this location. Looking down the peninsula toward Cherbourg, we could see a peaceful looking forest in the distance.

We searched the five Germans for intelligence, souvenired them, and then held a conference. We discussed whether we had come close to the edge of the German force and, being only three men and a Jeep, should report back to corps headquarters—or not and go on. We went back.

Our assessment proved accurate. While driving back to St. Mere Eglise, we met another corps officer Bill knew driving toward the peninsula. We told him of our conclusion. Unfortunately, he decided to continue. He and his driver never returned.

In one less eventful but unique reconnaissance, we were traveling down a road in the Jeep. By this time, Bill had taken over as driver with me in the passenger's seat and the lieutenant in the back like a VIP.

We were clipping along on a low-traffic road, still within known friendly territory, when a large metal nut dropped into Bill's lap. He picked it up, asked us what it was, and said, "Is this the nut for the steering wheel?" With that he placed his palms behind the wheel and popped the wheel toward his chest to see if it was. It was. The wheel came off. We had no steering.

For the second time in the war, I jumped out of a moving combat vehicle into a ditch, this time with only two other officers. The Jeep went on down the road without us. It finally slowed and stopped in a crash with minimal damage. I, and I suspect the others, always made sure the steering wheel nut was tight on every Jeep thereafter.

As we drove around Normandy searching for the enemy's lines, Bill noted that our GI's dug foxholes to live in and protect themselves from flying debris, enemy fire, and the elements. They dug holes, stuffed the bottoms with straw, and covered the tops with boards or branches. We agreed the holes were so numerous in areas that it looked like the earth had chickenpox.

Breakout of Normandy. We watched the operational plan develop and go into effect for the breakout of the Normandy perimeter, codenamed Operation Cobra, July 25 - 31, 1944. On July 25, after almost 50 days hemmed up in the Normandy Beachhead, a sky full of heavy bombers came over from England and blew a gap in the German lines. I was there in an observation post just behind our lines.

The bombs made a tremendous freight-train sounding racket. A huge cloud of dust rose in the air and drifted slowly over our lines. The dust confused the targeting process. When we identified individual explosions in the clouds approaching us, we evacuated the observation post. It was a good thing we did—our post was destroyed.

Later I read newspaper accounts of the breakout bombing. None captured its horrific sound and the sheer magnitude of its power and earth-shattering obliteration. I remember praying that in any future mass bombings, the aircraft overhead of Americans would always be ours or those of our allies.

The breakout was a success but at great cost. Our forces took more than 100 casualties from "friendly fire," including killing Army World War I veteran General Lesley J. McNair who was in a nearby observation post. Until recently, he had been the Chief of Army Ground Forces for Supreme Headquarters, Allied Expeditionary Forces (SHAEF).

On the front page of the July 28, 1944 edition of *The Stars and Stripes*, the "Daily newspaper for the U.S. Armed Forces in the European Theater," was a story by Reuter Correspondent William Stringer, headlined "Americans Plunge West to Split Nazis, Column Dashing for Sea Threatens to Trap Half of Enemy on U.S. Front." In it he wrote, "U.S. First Army HQ, July 27—Scoring a complete breakthrough west of St. Lo, powerful tank supported American columns suddenly wheeled westward in a daring seaward drive behind German lines that threated to trap half of the Axis forces on the U.S. front." The German forces were squeezed and rapidly began retreating to their own border.

Leapfrogging Across France and Belgium. The 84th Fighter Wing leapfrogged from headquarters to headquarters, trying to keep up with the retreating Germans. We finally stopped in Maastricht, Holland, toward the end of 1944.

One of our first moves was to a big French chateau, a fancy place equipped with a real count, a baron, and a lot of their extended family. We set up unit tents in the count's woodlot. For the first time, I had to locate a foxhole that was handy because a canvas roof doesn't stop much shrapnel. In the snow, ice, and cold rain and mud, tents are downright unhappy places to live and work in—as well as foxholes.

The count invited a few of us officers up to his house for drinks one night. The count and his wife looked like plain, ordinary folks who had sophisticated manners and lived in a luxurious home the size of a city block in Waverly. When the family entered the sitting room, they shook hands with us down the line, even the children. Near as I could tell, they owned the entire countryside, now not very prosperous because of the war.

A few weeks earlier, the Germans had lined the count up against a wall for execution and, for whatever reason, decided not to shoot him. He clearly did not like "Le Boche." (That was a French slur for Germans, meaning, in polite terms, thickheaded, disagreeable, and troublesome.) We quickly exhausted our smiling and limited vocabulary to communicate with each other.

We heard reports of a gang of 50 or so Germans hiding in the hilly woods in the area of the count's estate. They didn't seem to be bothering anyone. We figured they were trying to make their way back home, like the rest of the retreating Nazis.

The concern was that they might come out and be dangerous if they became hungry enough or if the Free French drove them out—at that time, the French weren't taking prisoners. There was a lot of hilly country for the Germans to hide in, requiring a small campaign to dig them out. The gang was never a problem, and we had to move on.

Driving forward on the ground toward Maastricht, we saw the effects of the Allied Air Forces. When Jerry got in a hurry to leave that section of the country, he had to come out on the roads in daylight. Most German soldiers moved out on foot across the fields toward the German border and home. But the German mechanized units left burned trucks, cars, tanks, guns, and other equipment in roadside ditches or pulled off into fields to clear the way for retreat. Hundreds of wrecks were scattered along the roads. Retreat without your army's air cover is an ugly business.

While crossing France, I flew reconnaissance and combat missions on loan to other units. On August 13, I flew a Cub for most of the day over our rear areas in a memorable mission for Allied engineering personnel. They were interested in checking the damage to communications, so we followed the paths of the various battles. From the air, the damage looked like the path of a large tornado cutting strips of destruction through the countryside, not touching either side of the strips. Whenever our forces ran up against a German strongpoint, the whole area was churned into rubble by our guns and bombs. Railroad yards were blown to hell—just wiped off the map.

During this time, two of our 84th Wing members got time off to go to Paris earlier than they would have liked—too close after the German's surrender of their Paris garrison on August 25. Our guys reported Paris was *hog wild*. The troops who entered Paris first were French, made up of French, colonial, and otherwise who could be recruited by the Free French, and equipped and supplied with American stuff. They weren't well organized themselves, so the general result was a madhouse with lots of drunks and lots of shooting.

Our guys were chased in and out of houses, forced to drink with everybody, had their cigarettes taken away, were kissed by all the females and half the males, and were shot at by snipers. They considered it a bad visit until they both came back alive to talk about it.

I managed a two-day visit to Paris later as the city was settling down. But Paris was still nuts. The city was long on wine, short on bottles to hold the wine, and short on food. Cattle were driven right into the middle of Paris for slaughter (no transportation). It seemed like Paris had a million bicycles of sorts, all kinds of funny peddling contraptions, and coal- and wood-burning cars.

Truckloads of bristling Free French with guns raced around the streets, looking like they were going to break into warfare any minute. The whole place was in a don't-give-a-damn state of mind. Remarkably, Paris, itself, was practically untouched by the fighting—best I could tell, just a few minor bullet holes in spots.

A big shot in the French underground movement took a Jeep-load of us Americans to his home in Paris for drinks. He dug the drinks out of his cellar floor where he had hidden them from the Germans, saying they were strictly pre-war Grade-A wine and champagne. He had used his cellar to hide downed Allied pilots and shuttle them to Spain before the invasion. Although I was no judge of good wine or champagne, drinking with him made all taste fine, and we got pleasantly plastered.

Our host had a toddler two year's old who looked a bit small and washed out. One of the Americans in our Jeep promised to ship a case of US Army canned milk to our host when he got back to his unit. I hoped he kept his promise because the toddler certainly looked like she could use it.

I spent one night in a Paris hotel commandeered by the US Army—it had hot showers, good beds, good wine, and C-Rations cooked by French cooks. Such luxury made the trip worthwhile. Outside the hotel, the Paris night had sporadic gunfire from straggling Germans, scared sympathizers, and belligerent Free French fighters still sorting out who was in charge.

During our 84th Wing's leapfrogging, our egg-hungry soldiers organized routes to buy or barter for fresh eggs from the locals. They quickly found new routes at each stop.

In one stop, three of us picked up a Jeep to load up on eggs for the officers, swapping soap and cigarettes for them—a lot cheaper than money. One bar of soap was worth all the eggs on the place and maybe a chicken or two. The problem was that at almost every farmhouse, when they found out we were Americans buying eggs, they invited us in and poured an assortment of drinks down us, both good and bad. We finally had to stop the trip because we couldn't refuse the drinks without hurting their feelings. We also brought back cabbage, lettuce, tomatoes, apples and a gallon of wine. We only broke 24 eggs on the trip back to headquarters—pretty good for the condition we were in.

In the process of our moves, I decided the heavy .45-caliber pistol I carried was a burden out of proportion to its usefulness. I bought a small-caliber gun at the Browning Gun Factory in Liege to serve as my "security blanket." There I ran into a sergeant with a dozen .45-caliber pistols strung on a coat hanger that he bought for $11 each. He would rub them in the dirt, take them back one troop echelon from the frontlines into the quartermaster area, and sell them. The going rate for those battlefield souvenirs was $85 each.

Throughout our movement, I was detailed to various fighter groups temporarily to fly combat missions, one time for a week. When we weren't flying missions that week (due to weather), I whittled while we swapped flying stories. That was the first time in months that I felt like a 100-percent flying officer.

Once we flew out of a large German airfield with bomb marks all over its runway, destroyed hangars, and burned airplanes and equipment piled around, either burned by our attacks or by the Germans as they pulled out. We met no resistance except for the occasional sniper fire.

By September 1944, the Luftwaffe wasn't showing its nose around our part of the French countryside, lately, not even at night. The once or twice it tried to put up an argument in force had gone badly for them.

I had drawn my first Air Medal for 10 combat sorties in World War II by September 26.

Meanwhile, I knew Child Number Two, Patrecia Ellis (Patty) Slayden, had been born in Avon Park, Florida, and that all was well with mother and child. I got the letter in late July, but Caroline failed to tell when she was born. It was strange having a daughter I had never met and not know how old she was. As we crossed France, I finally received word in September that Patty was born, most appropriately, on July 4, 1944. *Weemsana* ran the headline: "Hitler Mourns—another Fighting Weems is born!"

In our leapfrogging, we stayed in buildings the Germans had used as headquarters, usually in good condition. But for a country boy used to a home with fireplaces or wood-burning stoves in almost every room—one who had just spent the last five years stationed in tropical Panama and the Arizona desert—French homes with small heaters in their rooms were cold. Almost as bad, most of the French hadn't converted to indoor plumbing. I caught a cold in the fall that stayed with me through much of the winter of 1944 – 1945. Once I was hospitalized for two days and taken off flying status for a week until I could breathe again. But wars don't care. So I took my nine pills per day and flew sorties.

In eastern France, we entered World War I country with towns that hadn't been so devastated by the current war. The French were friendly with a lot of staring and hand-shaking going on (the towns were not yet overrun with GIs). The children pestered us for chewing gum, candy, and cigarettes, the latter "for Papa," of course.

But the lack of destruction in the towns was deceiving. In one fair-size town that looked untouched by the war, the people told us that the conditions of a French town depended on the character of the German CO in charge. In many, the German COs controlled the populations with hangings and shootings. As the Germans were being driven out of France by the advancing Allies, some of the German COs lined up the towns' people in France and Belgium and executed them before leaving. Apparently, the COs wanted to protect the German Army stragglers coming behind them who also were running for home.

In October 1944, I saw a short film about the Liberation of Paris, unlike any short feature one would see in an American movie theater. The film showed French civilians in trucks or on foot chasing down and killing miscellaneous Germans racing through the streets of Paris. It was brutal. By that time I had passed through towns where French and Belgium citizens had been executed by the withdrawing German forces. I figured the film was in retaliation for the Nazi executions.

When we stopped in Maastricht, life was quiet, at first—in spite of the fact that scores of German V-1 flying bombs passed overhead bound for the Antwerp Harbor. The V-1, known as the "buzz-bomb" or the German's "vengeance" weapon, was an early cruise missile. It was a 27-foot-long flying "cigar" with stubby wings that carried a 1,870-pound warhead. The V-1 missile was propelled by a pulsejet, a stovepipe looking affair lying on its side on the top of the missile's rear end. The pulsejet made a buzzing sound—hence the missile's nickname. The Germans launched 2,448 buzz-bombs against the port of Antwerp and other targets in Belgium, only stopping on March 29, 1945 when the last launch site in the Low Countries was overrun.

Our antiaircraft continually tried to knock the V-1s down in route to Antwerp. Allied fire and random V-1 malfunctions downed a few close enough to break the windows in the former German headquarters building we had moved into.

While in Maastricht, the 84th and 303rd Fighter Wings reorganized into the XXIX TAC, commanded by Brigadier General Richard E. Nugent, as part of the Ninth Air Force. Our mission was to provide command and ground-to-air control over four, sometimes five fighter groups.

The war heated up, and we became very busy, as documented by *The Stars and Stripes*, Vol 1—No. 117, dated Friday, November 17, 1944, headline, "1st and 9th Open Attack, 'Mystery' Force Lunges into Reich; Patton's Men Enter Metz Outskirts." Overnight, for the first time, four US armies (Ninth, First, Third, and Seventh) plus the British Second Army in Holland and the First French Army in the southern Vosges Mountains simultaneously attacked the German West Wall (Siegfried Line), churning the battlefront "along three quarters of the Reich's western border...for 300 miles on a continuous front from Holland to the Swiss frontier...more than 5,000 Allied warplanes—massed bombers and fighters from the RAF and USAAF—thundered against German strongpoints and behind-the-lines areas." The same article announced the formation of the XXIX TAC with fighter groups in the attacks.

I was assigned Air Inspector for the XXIX TAC with my own section and was sort of my own boss. I traveled around to inspect units and found myself up to my ears in poop (unit abnormalities) all day long. It was a good job, but I had no idea that following so damn many regulations and so much paperwork could possibly be required of Army units at war. I also was surprised at how inventive units could be to get around those requirements...or how they just ignored them altogether. Tactical flying proficiency and creature comforts while at home base (however gained) seemed to be many units' priorities. Their first priority was a good one. But, in terms of the second priority, my job was to get units on the straight and narrow path legally and administratively to keep them out of trouble.

Because of the Allies' success along the Siegfried Line, powerful rumors began spreading that the war in Europe would be over soon—by Christmas of 1944. (See Annex VII - "Army Indoctrination Training for Redeployment [Humorous], 20 September 1944," outlining training required to re-civilize GIs returning to the US, on Page 119.)

It also was rumored (latrine-type tacked to the walls) that units would be sent directly to the Pacific—and not by way of the US. A GI wisecrack appeared on the walls: "I'm giving the best years of my wife to the Army."

Americans, especially those winning at war, love their football. "Daily Bulletin #80, Hq, XXIX TAC, 12 Dec 1944" printed the TAC's defeat of the Ninth Air Force—at least as reported by a newspaper in Knoxville, Tennessee.

"Somewhere in Holland [Maastricht], Nov. 26th—GIs Mop Up Germans, Then Clear Littered Cow Pasture for Overseas Title Grid Game. First they had to clear out the Germans in a major engagement. Then they had to clear the battle-littered cow pasture. Finally in that strangest of settings for a football game, the XXIX Tactical Air Command Maroons won the mythical overseas Army Air Forces championship today from the Ninth Air Force Thunderbirds, 3 to 0. The field was regulation, the players had standard equipment, and there were 3,000 GI spectators crammed into a hastily improvised grandstand which ran along one side of the gridiron.

"But that's only the half of it. Only 12 miles from the German frontier, the bitterly fought game was climaxed by a fist fight and played with the backdrop of exploding 'buzz-bombs' and the earth-shaking retorts of antiaircraft guns. Shortly before the game ended, a formation of bombers and fighter planes roared over on return from a strafing mission against German gun positions and enemy placements."

Chapter 5: The 36th Fighter Group and Battle of the Bulge

We spent the winter of 1944-1945 in Maastricht in the ice, snow, fog, and never-ending mud—one of the coldest winters on record. I used Johnson's Baby Oil on my chapped hands and body (especially my sore feet) and as aftershave lotion and hair slick.

The US Army paused for supplies to catch up. The Germans dug in.

In early December 1944, Brother Bill and I spent a night together 50 miles south of Maastricht at his VIII Corps Headquarters in Bastogne, Belgium. I won a few dollars that night playing poker in a building that Bill reported was blown to smithereens by Le Boche two weeks later. The Germans launched their Battle of the Bulge Campaign.

On December 16, an undetected force of 20 Nazi divisions led by panzer units smashed into and pushed back US forward positions near the German border in the Ardennes region, creating a bulge 40 miles deep and 60 miles wide in the line through Belgium and Luxembourg. The understrength US divisions had paused to recuperate on "The Quiet Front" while the Allies fought the main battle to the north.

The Battle of the Bulge Campaign began on December 16, 1944 and ended on January 25, 1945. The German's goal was to surprise Allied forces and recapture the harbor at Antwerp in the overcast, wintry weather before the Allies could bring their superior airpower to bear.

To seize the harbor, the German mechanized forces had to secure the roadways through eastern Belgium. The seven main roads through the densely forested Ardennes Mountains converged on Bastogne—the control of which was vital to the German's success. They made a mess out of the entire Bastogne area from December 16 until December 27 when elements of

Lieutenant General George S. Patton Jr.'s Third Army relieved the besieged American forces.

As the battle began, I was in Maastricht, packing up records and rounding up the XXIX TAC's equipment to evacuate the area in the event the Germans kept coming. We were between the Germans and their objective Antwerp Harbor.

On January 12, 1945, I assumed command of the 36th Fighter Group. The group was equipped with P-47 Thunderbolt, fighter-bombers and operated out of Le Culot Airfield, USAAF Air Strip A-89, a few miles south of Brussels, Belgium. It had been based at Le Culot since October 23, 1944. The first night of my command, I laid in bed and heard the war south of the Meuse River.

The 36th included the 22nd, 23rd, and 53rd Fighter Squadrons. Each squadron had 25 P-47's, and the headquarters had a couple of P-47's for my staff, including myself and my deputy, for a total of 77 planes in the group (the numbers varied based on the replacement planes on hand or required). We were under the IX TAC.

My codename was "Starlight." I named my command P-47 airplane "Pete the Pup," after the funny-papers cartoon series that gave my wife her family nickname, "Pete," or "Petie." Caroline was the youngest of five children by many years—similar to Pete the Pup in the cartoon, who was a cute little drag-along, tag-along character who always needed attention.

On January 13 on a mission for XIX TAC, my pilots and I banged away at a German convoy with fair results, including destroying a staff car I hoped was full of Nazi bigshots. That same day, pilots from one of my other squadrons caught 10 Luftwaffe planes over a Rhine bridge and knocked five of them out.

Then on January 14, I was on a mission with one of my squadrons that wiped out a Le Boche airbase in Germany about the size of our own. We caught the Huns "with their pants down," so to speak, and really worked them over. We put on quite a show and left the ground covered in burning airplanes, buildings and such. The sky was full of our airplanes and the German's smoke.

In the first two days of my command, I had a whole group of self-styled heroes strutting around like they had just won the war. I concluded I had one helluva group of fighter pilots.

My getting a group command in January 1945 was a much desired milestone. However, it had been months since I sat in the P-47 cockpit. But war doesn't wait. I pretty much re-familiarized myself with my airpower weapon during combat missions. That worked well enough for me to be a septuagenarian writing these memoirs.

The weather only gave us a couple of days' break—the Eighth and Ninth Air Forces couldn't attack the Germans in the terrible winter weather. Snow covered everything. It was cold, and the clouds were socked in at tree-top level. The AAF had dozens of planes parked ready at the ends of the runways, engines warmed up, pilots in the cockpits, ready to fly missions supporting ground forces being attacked by the Nazis in any little sky they could fly in. We tested the weather front with individual sorties, but the bulk of our fighting power sat on the ground.

The siege at Bastogne, including the 101st Airborne Division, was fierce. Communication was poor, so we had to stay tuned to determine, when the weather broke, if we could get into the fight or had to get out of the German's way to Antwerp.

When the weather broke, the 36th Group finally joined the fight at Bastogne, but not in force. We flew mop-up missions: reconnaissance and close support. By that time, General Patton's Third Army had stopped the German attack on the southern flank.

Brother Bill gave the winter weather credit for keeping the German Air Force off their backs during the siege at Bastogne. He lost that argument with me. At that point, the Luftwaffe had no serious strength left on the Western Front.

About that time, Bill did some shooting, ducking, and dodging in two scraps, but that's his yarn. (See Annex VIII - "Tiptoeing through a Nazi Minefield at Brest and 'Task Force Slayden' near St. Vith" on Page 124.)

Bill Slayden became the G-2 of the 11th Armored Division on January 7, 1945, jumping from the Battle of the Bulge into a division on the move with General Patton's Third Army until the end of the war in Europe. In a letter dated 10 January, Bill quipped, "Haven't had a bath in so damn long and with no prospects of same in the near future that I've almost forgotten how one goes about performing the act."

In 1941 while I was in the 24th Pursuit Squadron in Panama, two of my remarkable bosses, Captain Roger James Browne and LtCol. Otto Paul Weyland, had commanded the 16th Pursuit Group back-to-back. In World War II, they served General Patton well. Colonel Browne partnered with Major General Weyland, commander of the XIX TAC, Ninth Air Force, as Weyland's chief of staff. They formed a high-performing air support team from May 1944 until the end of the war. The TAC gained fame for providing air cover for Patton's Third Army's devastating drive into Germany in the spring of 1945, including the 11th Armored Division. Patton called Major General Weyland "The best damn general in the Air Corps." Weyland retired as a general, and Roger Browne, my lifelong friend, retired as a major general. Incredible leaders out of the 24th Squadron's headquarters.

Writing to Mother and Dad in a letter dated January 21, 1945, Bill described his new job as G-2: "I'm much nearer the fighting now, and as you have probably seen by the papers, we are doing so much of it that I hardly have time to write. When this armored division tears through enemy lines, it destroys practically everything in its path, and the wrecked villages and frozen corpses bear mute testimony of our power and determination in bringing this war to an early and successful conclusion."

St. Vith: AAF's Happy Hunting Grounds. With the bad weather gone, the 36th Group was in action again. Our missions were simple: quickly deliver 500-pound bombs on German transportation targets, roads, bridges, railroad marshaling yards or whatever TAC assigned us.

We then proceeded to St. Vith, Belgium, for our allotted bombing time over the "Happy Hunting Grounds." St. Vith was a vital road junction near a valley in the Ardennes, a bottleneck for most of the German forces retreating in the Battle of the Bulge. The area was saturated with Allied aircraft 24-hours-a-day. A German Army was destroyed at St. Vith in a week.

I flew three P-47 missions at St. Vith. In eight-plane formations, we came in over St. Vith at or above 9,000 feet. That was an important altitude, one that was easy for pilots to remember.

It took a German 88-mm antiaircraft battery nine seconds to read our altitude, cut the fuse, load the shell, aim, and deliver explosives to 9,000 feet. Odds were heavily on our side as long as we didn't fly straight for nine seconds.

Heavy antiaircraft fire was much more of a problem for the bombers flying in close order drill. But by this time, the bombers had reduced St. Vith to powdery rubble.

At St. Vith, we circled, working down to 6,000 feet with ever-increasing gyrations. At 5,000 feet over St. Vith, light antiaircraft fire created a thin, gray German-made cloud. The cloud was self-destructing automatic antiaircraft fire.

The Germans had moved in tons of guns, and the altitude below 5,000 feet was streaked with tracers and terribly polluted. We dived into it and shot at anything that moved and any place that looked suspicious until we ran short of ammunition or fuel.

The Germans left miles of burned equipment to rust on the roads and in the fields around St. Vith in our three days of bombing flights. Several of my group's planes didn't come back, and most had battle damage, including mine. Getting shot at was normal, getting hit was somewhat regular, and getting shot down was unusual.

No German aircraft opposed our daylight operations, but the concentration of antiaircraft guns was enough to give war a bad name.

As documented in the 36th Group Historical Data: "The 36th Fighter Group, IX TAC, received a Presidential Citation on 22 January 1945 [for the group's efforts at St. Vith], per General Order 14.

"462 sorties were flown during this month [January], mainly against the retreating forces of Field Marshal von Rundstedt. This month the Group started using [bombs under radar control] through overcast (Pickle-barrel Missions). [Pickle barrel missions had the accuracy to land bombs in an area the size of the opening of a pickle barrel.]

"Close liaison between the ground forces and Group were in order this month as key personnel for each service played host to the other to better understand how the units functioned..."

We spent part of our time sitting on the German border in several inches of snow, wishing the weather were better. Finally, we were able to fly an assortment of interdiction missions, hitting railroads, road junctions, river traffic—whatever and wherever. We spent hours on end, circling Happy Hunting Grounds, keeping everything still on the ground.

Innovative Bombing. The Urft and Schwammenauel Dams, two of seven along the Roer River in Germany, controlled flooding in a large area and impeded the Allies' battle planning to cross the river in Operation Grenade.

The objective was to either seize the two dams or blow them up to control the timing of the flooding. The Allies finally crossed the Roer in Operation Grenade on February 23, 1945 after the flood waters of the river (released by the Germans) had subsided enough; the Allies had been delayed for two weeks. This marked the beginning of the Allies' invasion of Germany.

But before First Army units crossed the Roer River, the AAF was determined to destroy the dams. Bombing missions to take them out had been unsuccessful. The Schwammenauel Dam was a handy 50 miles away from our Le Culot Field. The 36th Group's P-47's had tossed 500-pound bombs at the dam and then tossed more to no avail. Word arrived that getting a dam was good for a month of Rest and Relaxation (R & R) on the Mediterranean Sea at Marseille, France.

We devised an innovative plan to take out the dam: strap big bombs on little-bomb planes. During the war, P-47's could carry 500-pound bombs and later 1,000-pound bombs in its shackles. But the bombers we were escorting already pounded that Roer River dam with 1,000-pound bombs, also to no avail. So, we reasoned that if we could hang one 2,000-pound bomb on each P-47 wing, take off smoothly, and fly carefully over German territory with no Allied forces below that we could make it to the dam to drop our added tonnage. So we tried it.

We set up an overload test takeoff on the smoothest runway available. The takeoff was 50 percent successful. That is, halfway down the runway, both bomb shackles broke, the airplane jumped into the air safely, and the 4,000 pounds of explosives, not yet armed, did not explode. *However*, those bombs went bouncing, galloping and careening across the airfield and threatened to wipe us out anyway. Shortly, the armament people heard about our experiment and came and took away our two 2,000-pound bombs. That was the end of that.

The P-47 had a good combat reputation. It was well constructed with heavy armor plating to protect the pilot. Coming back from a mission with battle damage was fairly common. I brought planes back five times with battle damage. But the battle damage to my P-47 in one run at the Roer River dam left an impression on me.

That day I was on a dive bombing run; antiaircraft fire hit one of my propeller blades, making a shattering noise. Absolute chaos ensued: my visibility disappeared and the world looked like encrypted television. I pushed levers back and forth and turned switches on and off until I got enough control of the plane to shakily fly back to base.

On the ground inspecting the damage, I was surprised, given the effects the damage had caused. Only a medium-size chunk of metal was missing from one propeller blade.

On February 22 and 23, the group flew missions in Operation Clarion supporting the First Army's crossing of the Roer River in Operation Grenade. More than 3,500 bombers and 5,000 fighters launched combined attacks in strategic bombing for maximum effects (ME) on the German communication networks and transportation systems across the length and breadth of the country. Targets included rail stations, barges, docks, and bridges.

Recorded in the 36th Group Historical Data: "138 missions were flown on 21 of the 28 days in the month of February, totaling 1198 sorties. On 22 February, 153 sorties were flown in support of the First Army's push across the Roer River.

"On 23 February, 51 P-47's escorted a flight of medium bombers to targets east of the Roer River in Germany. Our fighters each carried two 500-pound GP [general purpose] bombs to add tonnage on the bombers targets. This day saw the combined strength of the RAF, 8th AF, 9th AF, and 15th AF concentrated against Nazi Germany, an overwhelming display of air superiority.

"On 25 February, the Commanding General, IX Tactical Air Command [Major General Elwood Quesada] inspected the 36th Group installations and expressed considerable satisfaction with his findings."

Also in February, we bombed German targets deep into hostile territory, if for no other reason than to prevent movement on the ground and be sure no German aircraft could come calling. Occasionally, Allied airplanes that had been shot up limped in to our Le Culot Airfield because it was just across the German border in Belgium. Most of them had big holes in them—several carried dead crewmembers. (We weren't allowed to talk or write about Allied planes landing with dead crewmembers onboard during the war.)

In our air combat missions over Germany, every so often the German gunners on the ground reminded us they were still down there trying. In our first mission over the Rhineland, we ran into antiaircraft fire above 9,000 feet. Thereafter, I had the group use a light bomber's technique: fly a circular motion, 500 feet up, 500 feet to the right, 500 feet down, 500 feet to the left and add a little turn to first one side and then the other.

It worked like the light bomber boy told me it would. In that sky with every aircraft making like dry leaves in a high wind, if you flew a straight flightpath, you drew fire like ants at a picnic.

In early March 1945, we began moving from Le Culot to an airfield, Site Y-46, on the outskirts of Aachen inside the Germany border, an area under Allied control. This move was the first *voluntary* landing of American combat airplanes in Germany. On March 10, reporters and photographers were on the ground waiting for the first P-47, flown by Major Richard W. LaRoque from my 23rd Squadron, to land near Aachen. By late March, the rest of the group closed on the Aachen Airfield. It was the first time we lived among the Germans.

In the process of moving to the airfield near Aachen, I uncovered some noncombat peculiarities of the 36th Fighter Group—in other words, a couple of unit abnormalities I found as an Air Inspector for the XXIX TAC. A captain, one of my flight commanders, had his own private Jeep with US Army markings. He bought it from an army sergeant for an undisclosed number of bottles of liberated cases of brandy trucked in by the Third Army from General Patton as a gift to the group for air support well done.

As a side note, I think the sergeant got the raw end of the deal. I can attest firsthand that drinking brandy as a source of evening cocktails or refreshment at impromptu poker games gets old, pretty quickly, regardless of the fact that you don't have any alcohol to replace it and haven't had for months. We were using the brandy to start our fires.

I added the Jeep to my motor pool where I also found four surplus two-ton trucks that joined the group on the confused beaches crossing into Normandy in months past. In addition, we had fifty 40-by-8-foot size boxcars on a railroad siding full of supplies we hadn't used at Le Culot. Some were emergency backup supplies not supposed to be used in normal operations. Some not.

We proceeded to fill up one hundred more of the masses of empty boxcars sitting all over northern Europe with 36th Group's materiel to help us move to our airfield near Aachen. Army supply sergeants in war are the same packrats I knew in peace.

I never could remember that captain's name who owned that army Jeep in Belgium. I did remember he was a damn good flight commander, a "Top Gun"—right before I forgot his name.

The Arts of Dive Bombing and Close Air Support. The primary mission of the P-47 was to chase the enemy away from our troops on the ground. A call from "Rosalee" at TAC ground control locating a "Bogie" (unidentified plane) or "Bandit" (enemy plane) in our zone close to troops took precedence over any other mission.

One time when we were returning from a mission and were 12,000 feet over Liege, the XXIX TAC called in a Bandit under the scattered clouds at 5,000 feet at Maastricht, about 20 miles to the north. It was a bright, sunny spring day.

Our P-47's were almost out of fuel, but we charged down full throttle at 300 miles per hour, prepared for a dogfight. We whistled in over Maastricht to find the sky full of P-47's, dashing helter skelter in all directions. It was dangerous, to say the least. If the Bandit hung around to see the crowd he attracted, he must have been impressed. I was. We never caught him.

When I first started flying, I was a pursuit pilot, a go-chase-other-airplanes concept. In Panama, I was a fighter pilot trained to fight off other aircraft. In the year of 1945 in World War II, I was a fighter-bomber pilot—a fighter trained to ensure air superiority by fighting off the attacking enemy and a dive bomber to add "artillery" punch close to our frontline troops.

Dive bombing is part of the art of flying. However, in 1945, dive bombing, American AAF's style, had recognizable limitations. It takes an airplane flying relatively slowly or with fancy equipment to dive bomb accurately. Three hundred miles per hour headed down is not "slow," but it was the official speed of the dive bombing procedures of the day. It generated tales of "compressibility," otherwise identified as a manner of flying in which the airplane refuses to take instructions from its pilot.

The P-47 was not slow for its time, and it did not have any special dive bombing equipment. We had a gunsight casting a reflection on the windshield glass calibrated for our eight .50-caliber machineguns in combat.

Our group experience dive bombing in Germany determined our most effective procedures for the P-47. We started a dive at 45 degrees, well above the level in which antiaircraft cut in, pressed the attack straight into the 4,000-foot level, and then initiated a steady pullout, releasing the bomb at the exact time the target framed in the .50-caliber gunsight on the windshield disappeared from view beneath the rising engine cowling.

Our dive bombing missions were far enough away from our frontlines to be sure we did not hit friendly forces. Marshaling yards, such as the one in Frankfurt, Germany, were the best for dive bombing. They had long lines of trains and railroad tracks to line up with.

Close air support (CAS) was another move altogether with our troops a relatively short distance from our targets. In World War II, it was an evolving set of tactics. CAS to within a hundred yards or so of troops was controlled by the use of colored smoke and ground-to-air communications. Early in the war, CAS effects were not good—friendlies were killed.

Then teams of "forward observers" were trained and organized to support CAS. They were experienced pilots sent forward to the infantry's frontlines to do the talking to and controlling of aircraft coming in on close support missions. That stopped us from shooting at friendlies on the ground. But we had another problem to solve.

Pilots came down on targets knowing the area they were shooting at was hostile and, therefore, executed various tree-top maneuvers until they got back over friendly lines, straightened out and regrouped or returned to base. However, friendly lines were not friendly to unexpected aircraft coming in from enemy territory at tree-top level. Soldiers tended to "shoot from the hip" at the planes. Odds were on the airplanes' side until bullets going 550 miles per hour passed the airplane going 250 miles per hour.

Occasionally, a soldier behind the frontlines "got shot at"—heard bullets hit and "enemy" planes coming at him. He aimed his sight and waited for the fast-moving aircraft to come over the tree tops. Too many planes were shot down or damaged by friendly fire over our own territory. We changed our procedures to ensure units deep into the formations knew that friendly aircraft were on their way into Allied frontlines at tree-top level.

My 36th Fighter Group combat assignments lasted three months in 1945, the last few months of the war in Europe. The German Air Force saved the bulk of its remaining airpower to defend the Fatherland from bomber attacks, limiting its activities on the Western Front to sneak attacks and night warfare.

Chapter 6: Fighting Over the Rhineland

The Allies had failed in a series of attacks on bridgeheads to secure a foothold over the Rhine River, dashing their hopes of winning the war by Christmas of 1944. But improved springtime weather encouraged commanders to get on with ground hostilities. We overran the Rhineland.

Bridgehead at Remagen. The Ludendorff Bridge across the Rhine River at Remagen, Germany, was captured by the Allies intact on March 7, 1945 as the Germans tried to blow up the bridge—a stroke of luck. The bridgehead at Remagen was the German's last line of natural defense to hold up the Western Allies' advance and our ground forces' chance for the first major crossing of the Rhine. Several German officers were court martialed and executed by the German Army for failing to destroy the bridge.

Securing this bridge allowed the Allies to envelop the Ruhr area, the main German industrial complex along the Ruhr River, a tributary of the Rhine on the Rhine's east side. Our forces felt a great urgency to protect that bridge.

The bridgehead at Remagen required Allied air cover around the clock. It was the 36th Group's turn at bat when the powers above spotted a large number of German aircraft being moved under cover of darkness to within striking distance of the bridge, just 30 miles east of Remagen. They were parked under trees with camouflaging.

On March 14, I was in a flight of eight P-47's circling a small German grass airfield deep in Germany, just south of Kassel, in the early morning hours when the sun rose enough to start shooting. Because our targets were hidden and camouflaged, we had to "poke" for them.

When the first two or three airplanes blew up, our formation developed characteristics of a school of sharks in a feeding frenzy with no visible resistance. For our own safety, we had to back out, line up, and take turns attacking. We ran out of ammunition and left numerous smoke columns in the still, gray dawn. The 404th Fighter Group took over after us. By the time we headed home, IX TAC had, had a big day.

The events were published in *The Ninth Air Force in World War II* by Kenn C. Rust: "IX TAC had proved it could defend the bridge on the 13th [of March 1945], and the next morning, its 36th and 404th Fighter Groups showed it could also prevent major attacks in one of the outstanding achievements of the period. The missions by the 36th discovered more than 50 enemy aircraft, mostly JU-87s [Stuka dive bombers] bombed up and waiting to takeoff for Remagen at the well-hidden Lippe Airdrome.

"They [the 36th] attacked them...with 40 500-pound bombs, 12 rockets and numerous strafing passes. When their P-47's left, the airfield was spouting smoke from numerous places, and 23 Ju-87s and one ME-109 [Messerschmitt fighter plane] were destroyed and 20 were damaged.

"Next came 12 P-47's from the 404th, which bombed and strafed other aircraft at the base. Their attack lasted 15 minutes, destroying 21 aircraft (mostly Ju-87s) and damaging 19, but two Thunderbolts (P-47's) mushed together and exploded in midair" (Aero Publishers, 1970).

The Stuka was a famed but by then obsolete 1939 German dive bomber. It had a fixed landing gear and could drop bombs with pickle-barrel accuracy but, likely, couldn't win a dogfight with a fleecy cloud.

Now on the other hand, the Messerschmitt *was* a dogfighter, not a bomber, not a fighter-bomber. One might wonder if the 36th Group's eight P-47's had come on the scene one-half hour later and met the Messerschmitts in the air...would we have become eight instant war heroes?

Nope. By this time, my 36th Group had highly skilled combat pilots—and had proved it the day before, on 13 March. As reported, "11 P-47's from the 53rd Squadron over the Bonn-Siegen-Attendorn area found 15 to 20 Messerschmitts acting as top cover for FW 190's [the versatile Focke-Wulf fighter/fighter bomber/ground attack aircraft] at 10,000 feet. The Fockers were ready to dive bomb the area. Our pilots attacked from 17,000 feet, so the Fockers jettisoned their bombs and participated in a wide-ranging dogfight. The Germans lost seven Messerschmitts for no loss or damage to the P-47's"

(36th Fighter Group Historical Data, March 1945). We cleaned up on 13 and 14 March.

The 36th Group flew many missions during this time, and several of my pilots were in dogfights with the enemy. But for myself, I never faced an enemy plane in the air during World War II.

"From IX TAC, MSG CEN NO. 17, TO: 36th FTR GP: Through General [Carl A. ("Tooey")] Spaatz [Commander, US Strategic Air Forces in Europe, USSAFE] *Quote* Note your message dated March 24 outlines results (dated 26 March from General [Hap] Arnold) achieved during period March 16 to 22 March. Results are source of great satisfaction to all. Such smashing aerial attacks coordinated with relentless ground pressure can only result in complete victory. Please pass my personal commendation. *Unquote* You deserve every bit of it. Signed Quesada."

Operation Varsity. The Germans put up a fight after our success at the Remagen bridgehead, so our Army dug in and regrouped. The British forces to the north pushed through the Low Countries. Then on the morning of March 24, more than 16,000 British and American paratroopers supported by several thousand aircraft executed Operation Varsity, the last large-scale (and most successful) airborne operation of the war and the largest single-lift airborne op in the war.

Commanded by British Field Marshall Bernard Montgomery, its objective was to help the surface river assault troops secure a foothold across the Rhine. He dropped the British 6th Airborne and two divisions of the American XVIII Airborne Corps on the east bank of the Rhine, a short distance behind the German lines to ensure the paratroopers could link up with Allied ground forces quickly.

Among the thousands of aircraft in the operation, swarming like bees in the sky, the entire 36th Group flew cover for Gooney Birds (C-47s) with bellies full of paratroopers from Brussels, Belgium, and into Germany across the Rhine. On that day, from my cockpit, I saw them all in one clear, peaceful, sky...unopposed.

We rarely flew missions at group strength—usually only at squadron strength, rotating squadrons. Laying on such a mission in Operation Varsity took planning, briefings, and time; in this mission, our operations in the air were monitored and controlled by TAC.

Friendly Fire Incident. The final line of the 36th Group Historical Data for March 1945 said, "On April 5, 1945, LtCol. Slayden was replaced as Group Commander," a little more than a month before the war in Europe ended. I was relieved from command because, in the late afternoon of March 24, one of my pilots most unfortunately shot down a British Mosquito, a small Allied twin-engine plane mistaken several times for a Messerschmitt during the war.

I had returned to base after a peace-seeking mission dropping surrender leaflets over pockets of resistance deep in the Rhineland to find my headquarters in an uproar. The staff and pilots involved in the friendly fire incident, including two of the eight P-51 fighter pilots escorting the Mosquito, were writing their statements of what happened. The American P-51 was a British-made, long-range escort fighter that usually operated at high altitudes.

On the afternoon of March 24, my 23rd Fighter Squadron (25 P-47's) was protecting a formation of US bombers, B-26 Marauders of the IX Bombardment Division, at approximately 17,000 feet on mission X51-1 in the vicinity of Colbe, Germany, 75 miles inside German lines east of the front at the Rhine River. The bombers consisted of three boxes of six planes and one box of seven planes—50 bombers and fighters in the sky.

My group intelligence officer, S-2, briefed the orders for the mission to the P-47 pilots the day before with no mention of other aircraft in the mission airspace. Telephonically, the S-2 later received an addition to the order from IX TAC, saying that "one P-51 with special markings" could be in the mission airspace. The S-2 ensured the pilots flying the mission knew that addition.

The afternoon of March 24 was a clear, warm, sub-spring day; the mission was routine until 5:05 pm. As written in the 36th Group's Blue Flight leader's statement, the Mosquito approached "...our fighter formation from 11 o'clock. It was very close and passed by and under me and to the left with its nose down. I thought I saw a German black cross on its side as it flashed by." Maintenance records show the British Mosquito had been retro-equipped with an American radio, but the Mosquito did not identify itself.

"When I completed my break to the left, I was above and behind the airplane. It was headed down and in a turn toward the bomber box." The B-26s were moving into close order formation for their bombing run, the formation in which they're the most vulnerable to attack.

In the Mosquito's sudden appearance and inappropriate movement toward the bombers, two of the P-47 flight leaders, Blue and Green, viewing the Mosquito from different angles, mistakenly identified a German black cross on its side, and another Blue Flight pilot thought the small aircraft was a Messerschmitt.

Initially, Blue Leader had sent two of his P-47's down to verify the Mosquito was an enemy aircraft, but when Green Leader stated over the radio that he also saw the German black cross on the small aircraft, Blue Leader then authorized his P-47's to attack the Mosquito immediately to protect the bombers.

The Mosquito was being escorted by eight American P-51's from the 435th Fighter Squadron, 479th Fighter Group, Eighth Air Force, but not in close formation. Neither the Mosquito nor the P-51s had identified themselves to the P-47's when they entered the bombers' airspace.

When the two Blue Flight P-47's began attacking the Mosquito, the Mosquito pilot yelled to the P-51s that he was being attacked. At that point, two P-51's flew down to the Mosquito's rescue, but it was too late. The Mosquito had both engines shot out and was burning and spiraling toward the ground. The Green Leader stated that the two P-51's passing above him "seemed to be chasing the twin-engine ship..."

Under R/T (radio/teletype) from IX TAC headquarters, the two P-51 pilots were ordered to fly back to our base to file written reports with the P-47 pilots and group staff. After the pilots landed at Le Culot (we had not yet closed on Aachen at that point), there were rumors that a RAF VIP was killed onboard the Mosquito. Eight P-51 fighters did seem an excessive number of escort planes for one small Mosquito. But details about the downed Allied airplane, its mission, and people onboard were immediately classified.

My higher headquarters also was in chaos after the incident, demanding more information every half-hour on the half-hour. The intensity of their demands was counterproductive to my sorting out what had happened. Headquarters even threatened to court-martial my pilots, but that would have been purely for show because the pilots wouldn't be convicted under the circumstances.

In 1985, my son, Russell, researched the March 24, 1945 incident at the National Archives in Washington, DC, under the Freedom of Information Act. All we could learn were the names of the pilot and navigator of the Mosquito Mark XVI NS 711, who were American lieutenants from the 25th Bombardment Group (Reconnaissance) "on an operational mission of an unknown nature flown with another command" and "reported missing in action" on March 24 after being attacked by friendly fire with both engines shot out (the pilot was later verified as killed), according to the 25th Group Recce's official History for March 1945. The report stated one unidentified person was seen to parachute from the Mosquito before it crashed.

Later, we were able to get a copy of the Missing Air Crew Report (MACR) related to the incident. The navigator had a note beside his name, "R.T.D," which stood for Returned to Duty. He was the one who parachuted out of the airplane before it crashed. We never found out what the Mosquito's mission was in the sky with our bomber formation.

During the combat phase prior to the incident, we were fighting over Germany's Fatherland, so the Germans had stiffened, and the war had heated up. With the little airpower they had left, the Germans fought fiercely.

So how hot was the 36th Fighter Group's war zone at the time? Hotter than any other group in the IX TAC. Ending a March 31, 1945 IX TAC official report: "Total number of sorties per group of the IX TAC for March 1945, 36th Group – 2,499...." The 36th Group was listed first with 518 more sorties than the next closest of the IX TAC's five fighter groups. Our group previously had earned the nickname, "The Fightin' 36th."

Being a fighter-bomber pilot in the 36th Group in the European Theater of World War II was dangerous business. According to the report by "Headquarters, 36th Fighter Group Historical Data, 1 February 1940 – 15 October 1948, Howard Field, Canal Zone, dated 19 September 1947....The casualty chart for 1945, as of 8 May [1 January – 8 May] showed 48 [pilots] MIA [missing in action], 25 KIA [killed in action], and 12 P/W [prisoners of war], a total of 85. The number per squadron in this category were amazingly close, the squadrons' having 28, 29, and 28 respectively [22nd, 23rd, and 53rd Fighter Squadrons]." That's 85 pilot/airplane casualties in little more than four months for the 36th Fighter Group that maintained about 77 P-47's.

The friendly fire incident by my group in World War II haunted me. I'm sure it haunted the Blue and Green Flight leaders and the two pilots who shot down the Mosquito as well, especially the replacement pilot. He was a lieutenant, new to the squadron, following orders from his flight leader. I always thought it was a shame that anyone brave and capable enough to become a fighter pilot in the war would have the legacy of killing an American pilot in the last six weeks of the war. I was glad to learn from the MACR that the navigator parachuted safely out of the burning airplane. The incident was a tragic accident in a high-traffic war zone that resulted in the death of an American pilot.

Years later (1984), after I retired in 1962, my son-in-law, US Army Lieutenant Colonel Jim Hollis (Patty's husband), an instructor at the Command and General Staff College, ran across a brief account of our March 24, 1945 friendly fire Incident written for a section of a book illustrating "trigger happy" pilots in World War II and sent it to me. My account of the incident is based on my original carbon copy signed statements of the four 36th Fighter Group pilots, my group staff, and the two P-51 escort pilots plus the official reports of the units involved in the incident.

After reading the excerpt from Jim, I quipped in my very best Tennessee talk: "Corollary I: The sun never, never shines up the same old hound dog's ass all the time!"

Jim, also a Tennessean, responded, "Corollary II: Not all general hound dogs are creative, just stumble on one spot in the sun; not all creative colonel hound dogs make general, but such hound dogs learn how to create sunlight in all their spots. Therefore, creative colonel hound dogs should *always* wear sunscreen on their asses."

I countered: "I have been retired from the military for more than 20 years now. Could I prevail on you to locate a surplus Insertion Device, Sunscreen, M1, Colonel Size?"

The Destruction of Germany. In late March 1945, I had an opportunity to reconnoiter on the ground a section of the Rhineland overrun a while back and now occupied by Allied forces. It was an area in a 100-mile radius that my group and other AAF units had worked over for the past two months.

Every place was smashed. We drove through a fair-size city about the size of Phoenix, but we only saw three natives. Most houses were completely wrecked. From a distance, many walls looked like they were standing more or less intact, but when we got up close, we could see right through where they had burned—they looked more solid because of the piles of wreckage inside. The streets were people-less and stacked with rubble except for a few roads cleared to get through.

In the countryside between towns, we saw a German with a cow hooked up to plow his field. We went to one town much smaller, about the size of Avon Park, Florida. We walked around for a while. The few Germans who still lived there stayed strictly out of our way in their houses—such as they were. All sorts of furniture, fixtures, and timber lay cluttered up in the rooms or piled around. Stacks of broken clutter had been pushed aside into other rooms or outside, covered in mud and water from the rain. I doubt if there was a complete roof in the town. The only place for humans to live was in a room or two left on the first floors that could stay relatively dry.

The only visible life were lots of skittish cats darting in and out of the wreckage—no dogs, chickens, livestock or any such. The town was so quiet that it was downright ghostly. I'm sure people were still buried in the rubble, but there was no one to dig them out.

Wandering around was limited by minefields (marked) and the threat of booby traps in the off-the-beaten paths. If the Germans kept fighting and this happened to all their country, it should be their last war for a long, long time.

When our 36th Group closed on the Aachen Airfield toward the end of March 1945, we were stuck with two long plowed fields for our runway that had been chosen by an Allied engineer with more energy than commonsense. The field made Panama's worst grass airstrip look like a pilot's dream in comparison. From then on, I expected the group would have trouble staying operational in the spring mud on impromptu airstrips in Germany. In Aachen, we set up in tents surrounded by dead German towns.

A couple of my guards caught a healthy-looking 30-ish German man wandering around close to our airplanes and marched him around at the point of a gun to me. I had him searched and questioned him. He claimed to be a farmer (or so he said, and we couldn't see anything otherwise). He was concerned about his crop field that we were using as our airfield. I finally sent him on his way after warning him we'd shoot him if he came back. We didn't see him again.

But the next day, another farmer came with a horse and started plowing up one of the squadron's living areas. He said he had the authority of the military government to work his land and that where he had plowed was his land. We almost had to butt him with his own horse to get him to leave.

We were hard-pressed to keep up with the advancing First Army. We stayed in a half-packed condition for fear of new orders at any moment. On one mission flying out of the Aachen Airfield, I almost ran out of gas just getting to and from the fight. Everyone agreed that the more we moved forward, the sooner we'd end this scrap. No sooner had our rear echelon caught up with us in Aachen than we began moving to Y-62 near Koblenz, Germany, on the Rhine.

In early April 1945, even the Allies were getting mixed up about who was doing what and where in the fight. We spent much of our flying time trying to be sure we were getting only foe in our sights.

Once we caught hell for blasting a German convoy. The convoy ran out of gas, our GIs captured it, and then we came along and smacked up the German trucks. Nobody was hurt. The GIs saw us in the air coming, figured we might not know about the last-minute capture of the convoy, and got away from it.

About that time, I talked to an English-speaking Luftwaffe colonel, one of our prisoners of war. He had been caught flatfooted by American pilots who did a number on his airfield in the fiercest job of strafing he'd ever seen. They destroyed 40 of his airplanes and didn't leave a single plane able to fly. I gathered that was okay because his mission that day was to knock out one of the bridges over the Rhine River protected by the Allies. He and his fighters had no real chance of getting through the Allies to do the job and no chance of staying alive if he returned to the Nazis with the bridge still intact. He seemed happy to be our prisoner.

Fanatical Nazis were getting rare as hen's teeth. Everyone claimed to be very peaceful with no desire to harm anyone. That, I supposed, would last as long as the Germans were frightened. Or...maybe they wanted us to move across Germany instead of the Russians, who tended to be harder on the Germans.

On April 2, as we were moving into Koblenz airfield, one of my pilots returned from being a prisoner in Germany with quite a story. He was shot down 10 days earlier, captured by the Germans, treated okay, and walked all over the countryside (under guard), trying to avoid the threatening American columns. A collection of 12 Allied pilot prisoners carried the guards' guns for them and slept together with them at night. The Germans scrounged food for themselves and the prisoners from farmers in the area and finally left the pilots in a barn to wait for the advancing American troops.

The pilots stayed in the barn for a spell, and, getting hungry, walked into town. The roads were full of German soldiers (not in any semblance of order) and civilians moving in all directions, most of them walking. One of the pilots spoke German and talked to several Germans during their trek. Most natives considered the war "kaput" (finished) and either were trying to stay out of the Allies' way or get home.

The American pilots were strafed by Allied airplanes and sat through a heavy Allied bombing in a shelter along with a few hundred Germans. The only time the Germans around them appeared highly disapproving was the mention of "Jabos" (short for Jagdbomber, German for fighter-bomber or ground attack aircraft). The pilots learned quickly to claim to be Fortress bomber pilots (B-17 Flying Fortress) to keep from getting their throats cut.

When the pilots got to the town, they talked to a German major in charge and demanded food and beds, "...or else when the American Army arrived...." The captured pilots got both. After several days, when the Americans didn't arrive, the major loaned them a car and gave them gas to go find the American troops, who then came back and captured the town (officially). I detailed the pilot's remarkable experience in a letter to Caroline the same day the pilot returned.

Through the end of March and until April 5, I moved the 36th Fighter Group to its new base deep in Germany near Koblenz ("HQ, 36 Fighter Group, APO #595, NY, NY"). Our group continued to fly around much of Germany, beating up trucks and trains with little fight from Le Boche. The Germans shot antiaircraft fire at us only twice, but their ack-ack gunners were poor types who were way off the mark. We had a few planes shot up, but it was a drop in the combat bucket compared to past experiences. (See Annex IX for the "Command & Staff Officers, 36th Fighter Group, April 1945" on Page 131.)

On April 5, 1945, after relief of my command, I was assigned to a unit near Paris, France. But my former commander in the XXIX TAC, General Nugent, summarily counter-assigned me to his TAC headquarters deep in Nazi

Germany at Brunswick for the remainder of the war in Europe. I was reassigned just before I was supposed to report to the Paris unit and wondered if I had been listed as absent without leave (AWOL), a deserter in a war zone, an offense that was punishable by death.

No MPs came looking for me.

Chapter 7: The End of World War II in Europe

By April 20, 1945, I was at the XXIX TAC Headquarters in a Nazi Army Barracks at Brunswick. It was a fair-size town with the natives moved out of our area that we surrounded by barbwire. It had nice houses, and unlike the houses we had seen crossing war-torn France and Belgium, many of them were undamaged. The barracks were better than living in tents in the mud, but the comfort of the billets was marred by a shortage of food that made poorer staples more palatable.

TAC business was slow. Higher ups evidently considered the war practically over, and they hadn't been pelting us with papers, requesting info in triplicate.

My billet was in a row of apartment houses across from the barracks that had been quarters for Nazi officers and their families. They had pulled out so fast we had to clear away their meal dishes, among other litter. Thousands of Russians captured by the Germans to be workers were moving around and looting items of luxury and everything else. We had to post guards to keep the Russians from hauling off our stuff and equipment after we moved into the barracks and quarters.

One day one of the wives who used to live in the quarters came back and asked to put a note on the front door of her former home to tell her husband where to find her when he returned. She didn't tell us how she thought he might be able to just walk into the USAAF's XXIX TAC Headquarters and read her note—but she was concerned that if he did, we might shoot a Nazi officer wandering around our quarters. We never saw him.

I found million Mark notes (German money) being passed around. The notes were worthless, even for the Germans. They were printed during inflation after World War I and hadn't been used for 20 years. However, suddenly there were a lot of them around. Apparently, Le Boche planned to make "somebody" redeem those notes at post-World War I prices—that is, of course, after they won the war.

I stopped sending packages home. There was nothing left to buy to send home, and the Army was checking outgoing packages for illegally looted items.

AAF Captures Volkenrode. In April 1945, the 1st Infantry Division accidentally stumbled on a large research facility intact hidden in a forest just a few miles from our barracks at Brunswick. By luck, the division had captured one of the top targets of the AAF's Operation Lusty (Luftwaffe Scientific Technology): Hermann Goring's aeronautical lab, the most advanced in the world, where the Germans did experiments and dreamed up the V-2 rocket. The Germans called the facility "Volkenrode."

Our TAC was aware that the AAF had teams fanned out behind advancing US forces, searching for that and other facilities under orders from General Spaatz, the USSAFE commander. Unbeknownst to us, for lack of posting enough infantry guards, the captured Volkenrode was looted and damaged before the AAF team could get to it—unfortunately, by GIs as well as German civilians. I suspected heads rolled for that. Ultimately, boxes of data and information from Volkenrode were shipped to Wright Airfield in Ohio.

A peculiar story came out of that find. Civilian scientists working on a new German capability at the facility overrun by the 1st Division reported back to work a few days later, requesting permission to continue their research. They didn't care who they worked for—they just wanted to complete their projects. As we now know, scientists, including Werner von Braun, came to America and advanced our aviation knowledge rapidly: from V-2 rockets to intercontinental ballistic missiles (ICBMs) and Saturn V boosters for the Apollo moon program. Some of the Volkenrode scientists went to Russia.

An Anticlimactic End. War for the Allies slowed down. On April 25, American forces had cut through the Wehrmacht divisions and, by Presidential Order, halted at the Elbe River near Torgau, Germany. On the other side of the river were our Russian Allies, meaning we had conquered the Nazis from the west while the Russians conquered them from the east—effectively cutting the Fatherland in half.

In early May, I was checking out a new airfield up near the front and saw several German airplanes of different types come in fast at treetop levels at dusk with their wheels up until the last minute to quickly land on our airfield. Propaganda had been air-dropped on Germany for Luftwaffe pilots to surrender at Allied airfields by flying in slowly in daylight with their wheels down, land, and wait to be captured.

One of the German pilots had his tennis racket and other valuables in the plane with him. I'm not sure what he thought—that he would be able to keep his stuff as a prisoner of war? But the "capturing" part of enemy pilots came second after all GIs handy souvenired the planes and persons. The German pilots wanted to surrender to Americans, not Russians, so I'm confident the souvenired pilot was still happier to be an American prisoner, even without his stuff.

The night of May 7, 1945, the word was out that the next day the war would be declared officially over. By way of celebrating, GIs cut loose at midnight with volumes of their assorted side arms firing into the air, generally making it unsafe to be out and about. Unit COs raised hell.

Victory in Europe (VE) Day, May 8, 1945, was a strange day. It was much the same as any other day for the last week—with only routine activity and not much of that. There was no celebrating. For all practical purposes, the war had been over for a while. I spent the day reading regulations, catching up on them. The first really warm weather came with the end of the war, as early summers are inclined, but with nothing much to do. We had an officers' club available, but even it had no business above normal. A quiet end to war.

For the first time since I came into the European Theater, we officially went on a schedule that allowed for days off to "relax." But it was too close to the war's end for that.

My war had long periods of work and movement behind the lines with an in-theater-of-war urgency pricked by an edge of uncertainty and then bombing, strafing and firing on other people, Germans, who were killing, maiming or capturing Allies, my pilots, and destroying Allied equipment, my airplanes. It'll be hard to forget that.

The 11th Armored Division, with Bill as G-2, liberated the Mauthausen Concentration Camp in Upper Austria, on May 5, 1945 and then drove into Germany. Elements of the division were the first of the Third Army to meet the Soviet Red Army on May 8, VE Day.

A couple of days later, Bill reported he spent an evening drinking with officers of the first Russian division to make contact with the Allies. He drank too many vodka toasts, which he claimed he had to for the sake of international relations, and was summarily "decorated" with a Stalin Guards Honor Badge pinned to his right pocket flap. He said the badge later was quite a conversation starter among the Allies.

Miscellaneous foreign workers celebrated their liberation at the expense of the Germans. By a week after the war ended, we saw literally thousands of non-German workers (Russians, French, etc.) either living in camps or odd buildings and such or on the roads walking home. According to reports, they looted or killed Germans at every chance they got. American forces hired the foreign workers but kept them under guard to keep them from stealing any sort of commodity they could get their hands on.

By the middle of May, our blackout restrictions had been lifted. It was an odd sight at night after the last year of darkness. None of the German towns around us lit up. Allied units could be spotted like bright stars in the night.

GIs were lousy with rumors about the future that didn't seem to indicate reality, just a lack of anything else to do. The most accurate rumor, which we implemented, was a directive to start close order drills to keep the men out of trouble. High-level orders came down about not mingling with the local citizens, meaning mostly girls. The best I could tell, it wouldn't take much more idle time for the GIs to pile up an impressive list of courts martial.

On May 24, 1945, I flew west over the Ruhr Valley from my station in Brunswick on my way to a redeployment processing camp in England via Paris. The Ruhr was the famed German industrial area that had been one of the AAF's pet projects since the start of the war. I had bombed it several times. By May, the valley looked like one long series of bomb craters. Even the open fields in the industrial sections were chopped to pieces.

The redeployment camp was crowded with officers and soldiers awaiting orders with nothing to do. Some had been there for weeks; I saw a large number of long faces.

In early June, I left the European Theater on a war-weary B-24 bomber in England bound for Boston, Massachusetts, by way of Iceland and Goose Bay, Labrador. I spent the entire trip trying to sleep while stuffed into two sleeping bags to keep from freezing.

From Boston, I checked in with the Army and then made my way down the coast to Avon Park in Florida to my family, arriving June 17. I got reacquainted with my beautiful wife, Caroline, and our three-year-old daughter, Caroline, the Gremlin, a charming, chatty miniature of my wife. For the first time, I met my 11-month old daughter, Patty, leaning out from behind her mother, tightly gripping the back of Caroline's skirt with one fist, and peering at me with big eyes, the thumb of her other hand stuffed in her mouth. Little did I know that Patty and I would begin collaborating on these memoirs 44 year's later.

Post Note 1: The Slayden Brothers, one each in the Navy, Army and Army Air Forces in World War II, had their first reunion after the war at a massive Navy Day Celebration in Savannah, Georgia, on October 27, 1945. Commander Al, the oldest (a destroyer escort division commander, protecting American convoys crossing the Atlantic from submarines), CO of the USS *George K. MacKenzie*, DD836, had just docked his ship; Lieutenant Colonel Bill, had arrived back in America in August as the former G-2 of the 11th Armored Division, Third Army; and the youngest, Lieutenant Colonel Van, former CO of the 36th Fighter Group, IX TAC, had redeployed in June.

All three were alive and well. All had served the war effort honorably and attained the rank equivalent of lieutenant colonel. All were awarded Bronze Stars (or Air Medals) for their service. So they celebrated enthusiastically. The next morning, they made a pact to never recount to their families what happened on that night of partying with their wives and Bill's soon-to-be wife. When asked, they just rolled their eyes.

Years later, a report leaked out of one of them that might be the reason for their hesitancy to talk. Of course, alcohol was involved, and they didn't sleep a wink that night. It was something about being tipsy at Al's table close to the admiral's at the Navy Day Celebration for dinner on shipboard when, slowly, one at a time, all six of them began crawling around under their table, trying to find a hearing aid dropped by one of Al's friends, who also was tipsy and under the table with them. Suddenly, they realized the room was quiet and people were staring. And that was the beginning of the night. No doubt the wives and girlfriend were the only reason the Slayden Brothers returned safely to the hotel the next day. The brothers reported epic hangovers.

Post Note 2: An Honor Guard from the 101st Air Assault Division at Fort Campbell, Kentucky, 45 miles away, snapped to attention crisply, fired an 18-gun salute, and played taps for Colonel Phillip Van Hatton Slayden, USAF, at his gravesite in Wyly Cemetery, Waverly, Tennessee, on June 22, 1996. It was unusually hot that day, and sweat ran down the faces of those young soldiers in long-sleeve dress uniforms. They knew that Van Slayden's 36th Fighter Group supported their 101st Division at Bastogne, Belgium, in World War II, and their exceptional military bearing and professionalism honored him.

Colonel Phillip Van Hatton Slayden (1913 – 1996) participated in the World War II Campaigns in Northern France, Belgium, and the Rhineland and commanded the 36th Fighter Group (P-47 Thunderbolts), Ninth Air Force. He stayed on in the Air Force, serving, among other assignments, at the Pentagon, in the Central Intelligence Agency (CIA), as an Associate Professor teaching Military History at the US Military Academy at West Point, US Chief Advisor to rehabilitate the Republic of Korea Air Force after the Korean War, Inspector General of the Ninth Air Force at Shaw Air Force Base, South Carolina, and as Commander of the 4504th Tactical Missile Wing in Orlando, Florida. From first flying a PT-3 bi-wing, kite-like aircraft without brakes in 1937 to establishing the Air Force's (and America's) first Intercontinental Ballistic Missile School in 1959 while commanding the 4504th Wing, he contributed to the most advanced and powerful Air Force in history. Always a country boy, Van Slayden retired to his hometown, Waverly, Tennessee, on May 31, 1962 as a Command Pilot—having earned an Air Medal with Six Oak Leaf Clusters, three air medals for 33 combat sorties in World War II. In Waverly, he was a gentleman farmer, ran the Slayden Lumber and Construction Company, and managed Slayden Brothers' properties in the area.

Patrecia Slayden Hollis, daughter of Van Slayden and Editor/Collaborator of these memoirs, was the Editor of the US Army's and Marine Corps' professional journal, *Field Artillery,* for 20 years at Fort Sill, Oklahoma, before retiring in 2007. She interviewed for publication more than 80 senior leaders, including division and corps commanders returning from combat in Bosnia, the Gulf War, Afghanistan, and Iraq plus several junior enlisted veterans for their perspectives, a Sergeant Major of the Army, Chief of Staff of the Army, Commandant of the Marine Corps, and Chairman of the Joint Chiefs. She holds a BA from the University of Tennessee, Knoxville (1966), and an MA from George Washington University (1980), Washington, DC. Ms. Hollis was an Associate Professor of English for Park College in Parkville, Missouri, and an award-winning news reporter. She received the 1996 Katie Award and Statue from the Dallas Press Club for Best Magazine Interview with Lieutenant General John F. Sattler, US Marine Commander of Joint and Coalition Forces in the "Second Battle of Fallujah—Urban Operations in a New Kind of War," the Honorable (1991) and Ancient (1995) Orders of Saint Barbara Medals for service to the US Field Artillery from Commanding Generals (CGs) of Fort Sill, and the Commander's Public Service Medal (1982) from the CG of Fort Leavenworth, Kansas.

1936 – Lt. Van Slayden holds his nephew, Skipper Slayden, on his lap next to Uncle Major George Hatton Weems. Credit: Slayden Family

Nov 1, 1939 – A recently rescued Lt. Van Slayden walks past a row of P-36 Hawks at Albrook Field, Panama, after parachuting into the Pacific Ocean. Credit AAC

Dec 7, 1939 – What's left of a P-36A after Lt. Van Slayden crashed it on takeoff from Albrook Field. Credit: AAC

July 1944 – LtCol. Bill (standing) and brother LtCol. Van Slayden examine an unarmed Goliath, a German remotely controlled demolition charge, somewhere in Belgium.
Credit: Army Air Forces (AAF)

1944 – The Fighting Weemses—children and grandchildren of Joseph Burch and Elizabeth Rye Weems. Of Note: Commodore P.V.H. Weems, USN, (top right) went on to invent the Weems System of Navigation used by the Army, Navy, Air Force, Marines and NASA. Credit: Weems Educational Fund

Early December, 1944 – Lieutenant Colonels Van and Bill Slayden
observe the overcast weather in Bastogne, Belgium, shortly before the
Battle of the Bulge began on December 16. Credit: US Army (USA)

Winter of 1945 – LtCol. Van H. Slayden, commander of the 36th Fighter
Group, Ninth Air Force, stands beside his airpower weapon,
a P-47 Thunderbolt. Credit: AAF

March 1945 – Candid shot snapped of LtCol. Van Slayden, still in his P-47 fighter-bomber, after a harrowing mission over the Rhineland.
Credit: AAF

Oct 27, 1945 – Slayden Brothers first reunion after World War II at the Navy Day Celebration in Savannah, Georgia. Left: Caroline with husband LtCol. Van Slayden, Beth Merrick, soon-to-be-bride of LtCol. Bill Slayden, and Louise with husband Commander Al Slayden.
Credit: Weems Educational Fund

WWII - P-47 Thunderbolt was a single-engine fighter-bomber armed with four .50-caliber machine guns on each wing, five-inch rockets, and up to 2,500 pounds of bombs to support high-altitude, short-to-medium range missions as a fighter and be an adept bomber.
Credit: www.warhistoryonline.com

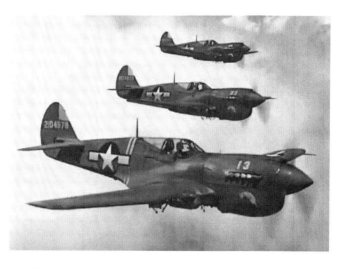

1941 - P-40N Warhawks of the 24th Pursuit Squadron fly in formation over Panama. Note the "Leaping Tiger" on the sides of the aircraft. The P-40N is the fighter plane Lt. Van Slayden piloted when he buzzed his hometown of Waverly.
Credit: AAC

Annex I – Backstory: Early 1900's Life
of a Tennessee Country Boy

The three Slayden Brothers were born at home, 108 East Main Street, Waverly, Tennessee: Alvin (Al) Weems Slayden (1909 - 1979), William (Bill) Marshall Slayden II (1911 – [2003]), and I, Phillip Van Hatton (Van) Slayden, the youngest, born on August 31, 1913 [died June 17, 1996]. Waverly was a small southern town of roughly 500 souls in 1913, including a half dozen Confederate veterans of the late unpleasantness between the states. All roads were dirt, and the water wagon made sorties to hold down the dust.

My father, John Alvin (Ab) Slayden (1875 – 1962), built a concrete sidewalk from our house across Main Street to reach the town sidewalk on the other side. The bump in the road it caused was no problem as logs were being buried at intervals along Main Street to hold the new-fangled automobiles down to the speed of horses and buggies. They scared the horses.

One of my earliest memories was watching my father's nose bleed profusely after the crank starter on the front of our new Model T automobile slipped loose and, spinning around uncontrollably, broke his nose. Dad gave up the automobile until my brothers Al and Bill were almost in high school and could do the driving for him—that was later in the 1920's.

In 1918 when I was five years old, I was playing when I heard a loud rumbling followed by a sharp pop every now and then as if a horseless carriage were backfiring. It came from the east side of town. Folks came running, and my father took me by the hand to see what the commotion was about. A kite-like biplane had made a forced landing in a local cornfield; its propellers were still spinning, making a loud whirling sound.

We rushed to see this new contraption up close, the first most had seen, including me. Dad, put me on his shoulders so I could see the plane. I was fascinated by it, and watching it take to the air after it was fixed was exciting. Little did I know how much of a role airplanes would play in my life. Unbeknownst to me at the time, that was the beginning of my fascination with new technology and love of adventure. The forced landing was the talk of the town for weeks.

Little boys wore short pants and went barefoot when school was out until school was in again. Several of our county schools (each one room) let out early to accommodate farm planting chores, but not the school in a town the size of Waverly.

Eating chips from the town ice wagon was a big deal every summer afternoon. "Eating" ice was hauled in from Nashville by train to be added to the cheaper "cooling" ice cut from our creeks in the winter and stored under sawdust for the summer.

The train also brought the daily papers for our news; only a few radios were scattered about town. The train had at least one passenger and one baggage car that arrived every afternoon and stayed overnight. That was an event in Waverly; in addition to people and baggage unloading, the engine unhooked, reloaded at the water tank, and moved to our man-powered turntable where the crew, usually with the help of locals, pushed it around so it would be headed back toward Nashville for the return trip the next morning.

The depot area, a vacant stretch of tracks now, was an active part of town with the Le Bond Hotel, several stores, and a blacksmith shop. It had become important enough to build a bridge across the creek to easily connect it to Waverly. The road to Nashville, 85 miles away, went the same direction as the train. But the road was dirt, and getting to Nashville was a dusty all-day trip— not much competition for the railroad.

Horse hitching racks surrounded the Humphreys County Courthouse Square in the center of town and our lives. Saturday was the big day when farmers came to the square for all-day outings—weekly gatherings to shop and socialize in town.

Gasoline filling station garages slowly replaced the five or six livery stations and blacksmith shops scattered around town. The last to go was A.J. Saunders' establishment across Main Street from our post office. He hung on by changing the front into a filling station while still working the trade with mules in the back.

The telephone had arrived at the turn of the century, and for a long time Mrs. Joe Freeman was the central source of important information such as, "Where's the fire?" "When's the bus due?" and other timely topics. She also was "central" for gossip. Dad, at that time, was a young fellow running a butcher shop on the town square, and his telephone was number "one."

Margarine came on the market white, looking and tasting like lard. Its color came in a separate packet, and you had to mix the two together to make the margarine look and taste okay.

Community progress came with a large, square white post with "Go to the Right" printed on each side that was planted in the middle of the intersection of Main and Church Streets near Courthouse Square. Constable Doss McCann stood guard for as long as it took to convince traffic that the sign meant what it said. When traffic didn't go to the right, he sent them back to try again. The mules, especially, were slow learners, and Constable McCann had to help lead them through the maneuver.

I was born after Waverly closed its calaboose. The calaboose was an iron box set of jail cells used inside a building to hold prisoners. In my early days, our two-cell calaboose was abandoned and rusting on the banks of Trace Creek below the Church Street crossing.

Inoculations put small pox on the defensive, and the local pest house for contagious diseases was abandoned where it stood below Hairpin Bend south of town on the road now called Cooley Street. The county farm, also known as the "poor farm," along Trace Creek west of town lasted for another 20-odd years.

The stage coach in Waverly had been around since before the Civil War when it was run by my Great Grandfather Whidbea White. He had five sons and eight daughters; all of his children married and stayed to populate Waverly—one was my grandmother Amanda Slayden. I was not only kin to everyone in Waverly, but also to everyone in Humphreys County.

The White's Nashville-to-Memphis stage coach tavern built of local logs continued as a residence and lasted a long time on east Railroad Street until it was abandoned. Later the original logs sold to a rich fellow who wanted to build himself a new old-timey house.

I grew up in a two-story house made of decorative concrete blocks painted white with a wrap-around front porch on Main Street, one block east of the county courthouse. My father, mostly a merchant, built the house in

1908. It had four bedrooms upstairs and one downstairs with a parlor, library, formal dining room, kitchen, and back porch.

We had extra fireplaces and wood stoves for heat. Electricity came to light bulbs in the middle of our 14-foot ceilings. When the electric lights blinked three times, it was a signal that a maintenance interruption was coming and to run get the oil lamps.

We had a bathroom too, and as far back as I can remember, it worked. Dad used foresight when he built the house, betting the city fathers would put in the city water needed for indoor bathrooms someday. But he may have had reservations because our bathroom had two doors, one leading outside through the back porch to backup outhouses in the barn, just in case.

The bathroom had to be large because one end was dominated by a wood stove harnessed to a large water tank that provided hot water for winter Saturday night baths, a standard procedure whether little boys thought they needed them or not. Mid-week cold-water baths also occurred. (Later, one of the bedrooms upstairs was converted into a second bathroom for renters during the depression.)

In the summertime, we slept with our back and front doors open (except for the screen doors) and our screened windows open to take advantage of the draft to cool us while we slept. Everyone in Waverly did the same—we never worried about burglaries in those days.

We slept on horse hair mattresses. Mother (Violetta Chapman Weems Slayden, 1883 - 1973) always preferred them, even later in life. The horse hair was taken from the mane and tail that is naturally hollow with honeycombing of a capillary system; the hair dried quickly when wet and was airy when you slept on it.

We maintained a big garden, barn, smokehouse, and hogs and chickens behind our house; the barn was occupied by our horses and a continuous string of milk cows, each named Maggie in her turn. Maggie provided the neighborhood milk—I milked a lot of Maggie's in my day.

We drank our milk raw, not pasteurized, and most mothers wanted it that way. Pasteurizing had a reputation for preventing the natural souring of milk, and everyone knew that healthy babies smelled like sour milk. Pasteurized milk couldn't be good for them—why the idea came from a *foreign* country. Even adults had to be careful because everyone knew that drinking sweet (pasteurized) milk while eating fish could kill you.

Our family killed a hog or two every winter—not my favorite thing to do. We killed them early in the morning in the backyard, dunked them in hot water to be able to scrape the hair off the skin, and strung them up to strong tree limbs to gut them, leaving them to hang out and cool down. The rest of the day was spent rendering the fat and cutting and grinding (and grinding) the meat until the hog was salted and put in the smokehouse—except special parts delivered to friends.

After a long hard day of hog killing, we were rewarded with a meal the likes of which I have never had since nor expect to find in any modern restaurant: fresh tripe and chitlins' with all the trimmings. It was *good.* The pickled pigs' feet Mother made each year was one of my favorites. We used most of the hog.

School and Borderline Juvenile Delinquency. With 1919 came grammar school for me, which at that time was grades one through eight. School was the domain of Ms. Maggie Tubs, First and Second Grades, Ms. Dolly Porch, Third and Fourth Grades, Ms. Kit Stockard, Fifth and Sixth Grades, and Mr. J.A. Gray, Seventh and Eighth Grades. They set up shop long before I got there and lasted long after I left.

I was seven year's old, already in school, when my two older brothers, Al and Bill, ages 11 and nine, took me on my first possum hunt. We didn't get a possum but found a case of dynamite, a common commodity used to clear land or kill fish in rivers, the latter illegally. My brothers found an adult who gave us fuses, caps, and enough basic knowledge to blow up local bluffs or tree stumps.

Blowing up stumps was especially entertaining. A fungus was sweeping across the country destroying our American chestnut trees, so the trees were harvested ahead of the plague. There were lots of stumps available. They often came with round holes in the middle that could be loaded with a quarter-stick of dynamite, leaves, and a suitable rock. We could send that rock straight up out of sight if the stump didn't bust loose in all directions.

We learned pretty quickly that a whole stick of dynamite was a *big* firecracker, so we used long fuses and ducked for cover. We exploded a dozen-odd sticks of dynamite just outside the city limits, grew weary of the sport, and gave the leftovers away. Our parents never knew about our dynamiting adventure—Mother would have had a heart attack.

School was not one of my favorite periods of life. Miss Kit gets special mention. She paid detailed attention to a left-handed boy who couldn't spell or read well. But she (and her ruler) were determined that, at least, I'd become a right-handed writer. I got a smackin' every school day. I was unhappy and frustrated. I got put back in the Sixth Grade and had to repeat her class. I cried—privately, of course. My grades seemed to get lousier every year.

Finally, in the Seventh Grade, my grades improved a bit. But I got caught with a key to the teachers' room. Mr. Gray told Dad, and he gave me a lickin'.

Years later, I learned I had dyslexia, a learning disorder I had compensated for by that time (but I still can't spell). Dyslexia was a disorder unknown in Waverly's schools in my day.

The school's assault on my left-handed handicap got mixed results. I never became right-handed, but I can misspell while writing with either hand. I became ambidextrous in the process and can sign my name with either hand. I am pretty sure my left-right skills helped me later when I flew fighter-bombers in combat. I know those skills helped me in fights. I could throw a surprisingly powerful right punch immediately after delivering a devastating left one.

However, I still get my right and left hands mixed up; for years I identified my right hand as the one with the my fraternity ring from college on it. In the car when my wife Caroline wants to tell me which way to turn, she says, "Your side" or "My side."

While I was in grammar school, the annual county fair, which had been held in the center of Waverly, was moved out near the new high school. The fair had traveling tent shows, medicine shows, small circuses, and funny dressed horse traders, called gypsies, who were reputed to be shoplifters and, maybe, child kidnappers.

Brother Bill and I were showmen too. We held "Chalk Talk, Stunt, and Magic Act" shows in our home. Bill told stories while he drew cartoons with chalk on a blackboard to illustrate the stories, and I did magic tricks. We charged a penny for admission. I wrote off for mail-order books on magic and props for performances in our house. I also did several card tricks in the show. I especially remember that acrobatic tricks were part of the performances.

Mine was to walk to the top of the straight-up stairs to our second floor, turn around at the top, and come back down, all while balancing on my hands.

As a teen, I once walked a telegraph wire strung across Main Street—on a dare. Mother never knew that either.

In 1928 I went to high school, and change was upon us. Empty horse hitching racks around the courthouse were torn down to make parking spaces for cars. Henry Ford's Model Ts were everywhere. Service for spare parts was not well organized—probably the fault of the customers. The customers kept using their Model Ts without replacement parts until nothing was left except the wheels, engine and enough frame to accommodate the driver. Then came Model As, and the automotive age truly arrived.

In high school, I played football (quarterback my senior year, scoring the most points), basketball, and baseball—mostly I was the South Paw pitching star. I was sure I'd be a college pitching star headed for the big leagues someday. Mother wanted me to become a doctor like my Grandfather William Marshall Slayden.

I also dreamed about getting work as a laborer on a freighter headed for Alaska and then jumping ship to homestead the state. I had read someplace that the government was encouraging it.

One night in my third year of high school, I shot several window lights out of the schoolhouse with a shotgun. I almost got caught doing it. Mother would have had a heart attack if I had, and Dad...well, let's just say that life as I had known it would have changed dramatically.

That was the same year I got good at pickin' locks.

First Jobs and Road Trip. When I was 13, I got my first summer job—other than family chores, which really didn't count. That summer, I went to work for a strange boss. Agriculture was the big business of the county, and that year my boss was point-man pushing tomatoes. Farmers grew them and hauled them into town where we processed the tomatoes for shipping at a temporary warehouse. With other elementary school boys, I nailed shipping crates together while the three high school boys graded the tomatoes for shipment. The grading jobs were easier and paid more money.

I nailed crates with the best of them, but being bored and because I didn't own a watch, I devised a way to tell when quitting time was coming. As the sun slanting in the window fell across the warehouse floor, I marked on the floor where it was when quitting time came. This told me the quitting time the next day—when the sun slant was just a little farther than the previous day's mark.

Three or four days into the job, the boss came to our crate-making corner and asked who had made the marks on the floor. I confessed and was trying to explain why when he promoted me. It appears he was short one tomato-grader, and I got the job. It never happened again, but in my first job, I got promoted for being a clock-watcher.

The summer before my sophomore year in high school, I got a job keeping track of the number of truckloads of gravel for construction of the Memphis-Bristol Highway, the first paved road in Waverly or the county. I made friends with the truck drivers who heard I had a pet Bull snake, a harmless snake that can grow quite large, three to four feet long.

Because of the blasting and other activities to cut the highway through the hills, the construction folks ran into many Bull snakes that summer. Before long, the drivers had given me enough Bull snakes to establish my reputation as "Snake Boy" and, in one instance, to become life-threatening. For a lack of a better location and overflowing with Bull snakes, I stored three of my larger snakes in a trunk in my bedroom—only intended to be temporary housing. Before I could find a permanent home for these three friends, Mother cleaned my room and, most unsuspectingly, opened my trunk. Without further explanation, that was the life-threatening portion of my snake-keeping: the life that was nearly scared out of Mother and the threats to mine if I didn't remove them from the house faster than immediately.

By the summer of 1931, the roads were improving; fords and ferries had to go. Brother Bill, about to be a senior in college, and I, about to be a freshman in college, worked painting a new bridge being constructed across the Tennessee River. One night it fell into the river—most fortunately we weren't on it at the time.

Suddenly out of work with pockets full of money earned at the grown-up rate of $28.50 per week, we got the family Model A and drove to Texas, the first time I'd ever been more than just out of sight of Waverly. Bill had a new college girlfriend, Pauline, in Abilene, Texas, and I had half the money needed for the trip.

Arkansas and Texas were one massive expanse of dusty roads and the same lifestyle we had in Tennessee, which was reassuring. There were no motels; boarding houses were common enough, but it was summer and we didn't want to waste our money on a luxury we slept through. So we slept wherever we happened to be when it got dark—no problem, except we got rained on a time or two.

We mostly ate at the back of grocery stores; you bought the food at the store and ate it at a stand-up counter in the back that had salt, pepper, hot sauce, and occasionally even ketchup. These were the 1930's precursors to our fast-food restaurants.

The roads were only paved in and around the big cities, except for one stretch of 20 or so miles in southwest Arkansas. The road was paved one-lane wide; folks driving to Texas had the right-of-way. So coming back from Texas, we had to get off the road for three cars. We went to Abilene to see the girlfriend and then south to the border of Mexico, so we could say we had been to a foreign country.

That Texas trip is best remembered because we picked up a horned toad. About that time, newspapers had carried a sensational story of a horned toad that had lived for 30 years in a concrete block in the foundation of a courthouse in Eastland, Texas. We brought a hardy one back from Texas to Waverly and incarcerated it with our names and documents in a hollow block of concrete that still sits in the side yard of 108 East Main Street, our home place.

We always planned to dis-incarcerate Ethelbert (named so generically because we couldn't determine its sex) and planned several coming-out parties. But distractions such as marriage, war, career travels away from Waverly, and, finally, old age have gotten the best of us. Besides, the story is better as a legend.

My Mothers: Violetta Slayden and Dixie Turner. Mother was an intelligent, strong willed woman. Her life was her family, and I cherished her.

Mother also was committed to our community. When I was a baby, our neighbor Paul May's mother died giving birth to him, so Mother took on the job of wet nurse for Paul, keeping him alive. Later Paul, who was always smaller and a great deal shorter than I (like his father, I might add), maintained I never let him have a fair share of my milk.

Buddy McNabb was a howling young'un in a filthy crib when his mother died. (Dad had hired his father, Ben McNabb, who was a carpenter and new in town, to work in a lumber company Dad had a part interest in.)

Violetta heard the situation was critical and walked two blocks to see for herself. She came back with Buddy, and he stayed several weeks with us feeding him Maggie's milk until Ben McNabb could reestablish his family to care for Buddy. Much later, after Dad had lost almost everything before the stock market crash, Ben McNabb met Dad at the train station when Dad was returning from a lengthy stay in a Nashville hospital and offered him a job and partnership in a lumber company. When Ben retired, Dad bought Ben's share of the lumber company that had flourished.

Mother also was bold. As her boys approached puberty, they felt the Bible Belt town of Waverly was overly restrictive for teenage entertainment in the 1920's. The lack of progressiveness and prevalence of gossip became too much for Violetta when the town criticized a teen-organized *dance* with her two older boys as ringleaders. (At the time, I was still too interested in fishing, frog gigging, and such.)

She had invited the teens to a dance in her home, using her piano and rolling up her rug in the parlor (the room set aside strictly for visitors) to allow boys and girls to dance together. Mother reasoned that she wanted those activities right where she could see them. Comments from the town's church pulpits (including our own Methodist pulpit) about her culpability in such a shocking event were more than she had expected.

Mother recognized the town was going through trying times. It had vibrated with shock when shorts replaced bloomers on the high school girls' basketball team—there was talk of abolishing the sport. Nevertheless, after her dance, Mother had very little use for Waverly's brand of organized religion, choosing to become a home-student of the Bible while encouraging her husband and sons to go to church and Sunday school.

Violetta Slayden was a founding and active member of the Old Reynoldsburgh Chapter of the Daughters of the American Revolution (DAR) in Waverly. She once traveled to Washington, DC, for a DAR Convention. In 1941 she went to visit her baby brother, Colonel George Hatton Weems, who was Chief of the US Military Mission to Haiti. Her trips were remarkable as few women in Waverly left the state, much less the country.

Mother affectionately called me "Puddin'" as I grew up. One memorable afternoon, I was in my early teens, standing (in a manly pose) with other budding sports lettermen during the Saturday crush at Courthouse Square. Mother passed by, looked up and smiled, and then said, "Hi, Puddin.'" I was destroyed. Waverly never let me forget Mother's nickname for me. When my grown children visited Waverly and met town folks, some natives would ask, "Now, are you Al's, Bill's or Pud's child?"

When Violetta got glaucoma (misdiagnosed) in her sixties and went blind over 15 years, she remained as independent and strong willed as ever—clearly the matriarch of the family. She lived alone at 108 East Main at age 77 after Dad died in 1962, the year I retired from the Air Force and came back to Waverly.

To help my blind Mother maintain her independence, I rigged a wire "highway" web on the right side throughout the house just above Mother's height. She reached up to use it to find her way and steady her gait, learning to walk through the house with confidence and a bit of speed. I also rigged the telephone so she could decipher the raised numbers and make phone calls. We boys bought her a Bible and monthly books and news on records for a machine designed for the blind. Along with listening to the television, Violetta stayed fairly current on world events and societal changes.

I was amazed at how much Mother had experienced in these United States during her 89 years of life. As the oldest child and only daughter, she lived on and worked the Weems family Barton's Creek farm in Montgomery County, Tennessee. The once-wealthy family lost everything after the Civil War and had retreated to the small farm. At age 13, she became "Mother" to her five brothers at the death of her parents, the youngest, age five. The Weems orphans stayed on the farm with little money and no electricity and grew or made everything they needed. Remarkably, she got one brother into the US Military Academy at West Point, one into the US Naval Academy at Annapolis, one became a lawyer and then county judge, and two were successful farmers in the area.

Before Mother died, she heard the television description of the first manned spacecraft, Apollo 11, land on the moon on July 20, 1969 where Neil

Armstrong and Buzz Aldrin walked the lunar surface and described their view of earth from space.

Dixie Turner (1896 – 1985), Mother's Negro maid of 50 years (nearly as blind as Mother), came in the mornings, cooked her meals, and left in the late afternoons after washing the dinner dishes. Dixie was a true friend and companion to Mother and almost as strongwilled. Occasionally, they would fuss at each other like sisters.

Dixie was a true Southern cook from scratch and the best in three counties. For summer Sunday family lunches, she would cook many scrumptious dishes for us: her homegrown fried okra, green beans, creamed corn, sliced tomatoes, mashed potatoes, fried chicken, Tennessee country ham, biscuits, cornbread, homemade fruit jams and pickles, plus her assorted cakes and pies. If we were especially lucky, we got to eat her wild blackberry cobbler with homemade vanilla ice cream we cranked for her.

I (and later my children) stopped at various county hillsides in the summer with a bucket I always kept in the back of my truck and picked wild blackberries for her. Her cobbler was *larapin.* (For you non-country readers, that is pronounced "lair-a-pin" and means a taste well beyond excellent.)

Dixie always spoiled me, the baby of the family, and praised everything I did. She also adored her boys, Al and Bill, and spoiled all our children. I loved Dixie for as far back as I can remember.

In 1954, after the Social Security Act of 1935 had been expanded to cover Negroes, Dad enrolled Dixie—which was a source of great personal pride for her. She considered herself paying for her own retirement. Enrolling her was no easy task back then because when and where Dixie was born and to whom were undocumented. Dad had to use reports of older witnesses and city officials with knowledge of her citizenship to enroll her.

The Slayden Lumber and Construction Company built her a comfortable and safe cinder block home with a fireplace down in the holler just south of town with the other Negroes. It was built to her specifications and on the location she picked. By my retirement in 1962, Dixie was too old to walk to Mother's house, so I picked her up early in the morning, stayed for breakfast with her and Mother, and then came back to drive her home every evening.

When Mother died in 1973, Dixie, 66 year's old, an old maiden lady with no family in the area, had lost most of her sight. For the rest of her life, I picked her up at least once a week to take her to deposit her Social Security check in the bank, go to the doctor's, or shop for groceries and supplies, and fix (or arrange to have fixed) anything broken in her home. When she was in her mid-eighties, I took her shopping list and brought the groceries and supplies to her home.

The holler could be a rough place to live; most residents didn't have much money or bank accounts, just kept cash stashed somewhere. Everyone in the holler knew Dixie, who carried a six-inch switch-blade knife and could use it, kept no cash at home and was under the protection of the Slaydens.

Until the day she died at 89 year's old, I was her support structure, the person she trusted with information about her life, health, and finances. I was a co-signer on her bank account. Following her instructions, I arranged for her funeral and bought the headstone for the burial plot she already owned.

I mourned her—she gave me and my family a lifetime of love and service.

My Father, My Model. The Great Depression in 1929 came in with a whimper. Dad already had lost everything. The road I had helped pave through Waverly brought an unexpected volume of displaced persons, and Mother hung out the first of several "Rooms for Rent" signs to make ends meet—those signs cropped up all over Waverly.

Dad had been a successful local businessman. Among other properties, he and his brother Lucian owned the 1,500-acre Hurricane Mills farm and mansion now owned by country singing star Loretta Lynn. But when the bottom fell out of the price of land in 1927, they were forced to sell the farm and other property. By the time the stock market crash came in October 1929, Dad was broke.

To add to his misfortune, he had to have a growth removed from his stomach and spent time in a Nashville hospital. Upon his return to Waverly, Ben McNabb offered Dad a partnership in the McNabb lumber company, helping to save Dad financially.

Dad, to his credit, did not take the bankruptcy for which he fully qualified. He chose "the harder right" and paid his debts in full, which took a long time. With such integrity and credibility, he had the confidence of those who worked with him and, again, proved himself an able businessman. Before he died, Dad amassed a second small fortune in farms, bank stock, and the

Slayden Lumber and Construction Company that he bought from Ben McNabb when Ben retired (which Dad renamed after our family).

Education was always a priority for Dad. Ab and Violetta Slayden saw to it that their three sons graduated from college. They then gave each of their eight grandchildren three $1,000 bonds for their college educations. All but one of their eight grandchildren earned college degrees, five have master's degrees, one is a Certified Public Accountant (CPA), and one has her Ph.D.

Caroline and I continued that tradition: we paid for five college degrees (our four children and one of their spouses) and three master's degrees. (Patty and her husband got master's degrees on their own.) In retirement, I served as Vice Chairman with Brother Bill Slayden Chairman of the Weems Educational Fund, headquartered in Waverly, established by the family in 1939 and endowed by our bachelor Uncle Brigadier General George Hatton Weems' estate at his death in 1957. The Fund originally provided interest-free honor loans for college with the recipients pledging to repay the loans for others to use; but it now awards college scholarships and supports educational projects, primarily in Montgomery, Dickson, and Humphreys Counties in Tennessee.

As Dad lay dying of angina in 1962, he instructed me that several older folks in town depended on him for a portion of their living and that support must continue until they died. One was a retired old Black farmer, a widower, who lived in a one-room log cabin on Billy Goat Hill with a fireplace as his only means of heat. Dad said he was "a good man." Each fall, Dad "lent" him the money to buy enough firewood to get through the winter—the farmer retained his dignity by "borrowing" the money, and Dad always played along. So did I until that old gentleman with the black milky eyes died.

Dad, a quiet, reserved man of kindness and integrity, always did the right thing, even when no one was looking.

Annex II – Backstory: College during the Great Depression

In the 1930's, Dad, who had never been to college, declared his three sons would, even though we were living in the small (1,152 folks in the 1930's Census) town of Waverly that was off the beaten path in the middle of a whopping big depression. Oldest son, Al, was the first to meet this objective by getting appointed to the US Naval Academy at Annapolis, Maryland. Middle son Bill hitchhiked across the state to the University of Tennessee in Knoxville and began college, eventually putting himself through law school.

That left me, still in high school focused on baseball and our family's Model A. I was the only one at home who could drive it, so I learned to double-date with fellows who could pay for the fuel. I had chores (milking Maggie, hoeing, killing hogs, suckering the tobacco, etc.) that I always had, so the big depression was "okay" from my high school country boy point of view.

When it came time for me to go to college, my grades had me well down in the pack. I didn't understand why I should go to college except that I'd become the "Black Sheep" of the family if I didn't.

In 1931, the summer before I was to go to college, a friend came to Waverly on a motorcycle on his way to a Citizens Military Training Camp (CMTC) at Fort Oglethorpe, Georgia. He invited me to ride along. I was always up for an adventure and wanted to ride to Georgia on the back of his motorcycle.

I worked out the details for admission to the one-month camp. It was easy to get in. Congress had set up Boy Scout-type military camps for unemployed young men to get them off the streets. Country boys like me grew up riding horses and firing guns—CMTC sounded great.

Fort Oglethorpe was a cavalry post, so we used the regular units' horses. We brushed them during the week and rode them on Sundays, taking good care of them. We mostly lived in tents and marched around. The best part of CMTC was the rifle range. It was pure camping up in the mountains away from civilization where we fired the World War I Springfield bolt-action rifle until our shoulders got too sore to shoot anymore.

The Art of Hitchhiking. At the end of that summer, after riding the motorcycle back to Waverly, I hitchhiked across the state to the University of Tennessee at Knoxville to matriculate as a freshman. More roads were being paved, so lots of people stood out by the sides of roads and requested rides by holding up their thumbs. For students looking like students, it worked better than a ticket for the train.

Hitchhiking Technique Number One: dress like someone, someone would want to pick up. I used to dress to look like a student or athlete. I sometimes packed my clothes in a banjo case to hitchhike; people were more inclined to pick up someone who could entertain them during the trip. When they picked me up and found out the banjo case was only a ploy to get them to pick me up, they felt entertained anyway.

Hitchhiking Technique Number Two: give the driver a startling thumbs up. I would spot a car coming toward me, do a back flip along the side of the road, and come out of it on my knees leaning back with my thumb rising. That technique worked well. Often I had to trot several yards to cars that stopped because the drivers were too busy laughing to stop their cars any closer.

Using these techniques, I saw a lot of Tennessee that I probably never would have seen. Years passed before hitchhiking developed a bad reputation and students had to go back to buying tickets.

On the road, when I got hungry and was down to pocket change, I ate like many ate during the depression. I bought a loaf of bread for a nickel and a can of pork and beans for six cents, oodled out the center of the bread and ate it (none came in slices in those days), filled the center with pork and beans, and ate the loaf like an ice cream cone. The menu was complete with water to drink.

After entering UT, I realized college is hard on a country boy who never cared for school. Two years of compulsory military Reserve Officers' Training

Corps (ROTC) was not fun, and I was more than 250 miles away from home. Marching around the UT hillsides in ROTC with a rifle on my shoulder had drawbacks, so I arranged to spend my sophomore year in the school band for military credit. I qualified for the cymbals, beating them to the sound of the base drum. I had no musical talent and was not included on the one football game trip the band made that year.

But the worst was UT had discontinued its baseball program. (It turned out to be a temporary suspension, but that didn't help me at the time.) For a left-handed, 19-year-old, high school pitching star, no baseball at UT was devastating. My problem was solved the next summer.

The summer before my sophomore year at UT (1932), my best friend, John Anderson, a high school football star, and I hitchhiked to UT where pre-school football practice was under way and "walk-ons" were considered. I was a member of the Sigma Nu fraternity, so we used a roof-window entrance to the empty fraternity house where we bunked while John went to football practice. He returned from the first day of practice feeling "so-so." Walk-ons tend to stand around and watch others practice.

However, a bigger problem faced us when we awoke the next morning. John's pants, his only pair, had been stolen with our precious $10 in the pocket—our only finances. We eventually found the empty pants discarded by the thief out on the roof. But the next sure meal was 250 miles away in Waverly, so we hit the road.

We were barely a mile from UT on the western edge of Knoxville trying to hitchhike when we decided we had to split up to get home. We were hot and tired. No one was picking us up, even on a corner that should have been great for hitchhikers. We flipped a coin, and I had to get out of sight until John caught a ride.

Right away a car stopped. John and the driver talked. John came and got me and said the driver wanted to talk to me too. The driver was a Mr. Ross N. Lillard, a lawyer from Oklahoma City, a native of Tennessee, and a Regent at Oklahoma City University (OCU). He noticed that John and I wore white sports sweaters with the big "W" (for Waverly) on them. Those wool sweater were brutal to wear in hot weather, but it helped get rides (Hitchhiking Technique Number One).

It seemed that Mr. Lillard, as he later admitted, had bragged inordinately to the other OCU Regents that when he went home on vacation, he'd bring back some *real* talent for OCU—Tennessee athletes. It appeared that he was on his way back to Oklahoma City, and the only athletes he'd found were John and I in our Waverly sweaters.

We rode west with Mr. Lillard and his young son for 21 miles until he turned south toward Chattanooga. That short ride produced two college scholarships, jobs supplementing the scholarships, two college degrees, eventually, a family for John Anderson in Oklahoma, and years later, his retirement as Chief of the Oklahoma City Fire Department, the place he started working to help supplement his scholarship.

A few days after we got back to Waverly that summer, a letter arrived from OCU offering us both athletic scholarships. John borrowed five dollars from me, left for Oklahoma, and established himself as a valuable football player for OCU, paving the way for my acceptance on a baseball, basketball and football scholarship the following year (1933).

Over the years, Mr. Lillard watched his Tennessee boys serve him honorably and always claimed a good day's work on that road corner outside of Knoxville. He remained our lifelong friend and advisor.

Nineteen thirty-three was also the year I learned to smoke. My mother's brother, then Major George Hatton Weems ("Uncle Major"), a West Point graduate who "lived and breathed" the Army, showed me how to roll Bull Durham cigarettes at the tender age of 20. Only rich folks could afford pre-rolled, store-bought cigarettes.

Much later in 1951, when I was relatively rich (at least by 1933 standards) as a lieutenant colonel in the Air Force, I had perfected my Bull Durham rolling technique. I could remove the tobacco pouch and cigarette papers from my pocket, open the draw-string pouch, spread the paper out, shake in the tobacco, roll the cigarette, lick the paper closed, close the draw-string pouch, put the pouch in my pocket, put the cigarette in my mouth and, finally, light the cigarette with matches—all with one hand. Admittedly, I used my mouth to help, but only to open and close the draw-string pouch, lick the paper closed and inhale the cigarette while I lit it. The rest was done one-handed. I was cocktail-hour entertainment. Friends would gather around, drinks in hand, and ask me to demonstrate my Bull Durham skills.

Adventures of a Hotel Night Clerk. At OCU in 1933, the funds provided in our athletic scholarships only applied to the school costs. We had to get jobs to live on. First I worked as a part-time night clerk at a small hotel for room and $2.50 per week. It was dull work, minding the lobby for three or four hours until 11:00 p.m. each night. But the hotel was close to a family-style restaurant where I could overeat for 25 cents a meal.

I soon discovered that night clerks learn a lot outside the lobby. The hotel had a spat of peeping Toms, and hotel security was my responsibility. I'd make noisy rounds outside the hotel to scare any peeping Tom into running out of the dark alley, which he did. He ran, I chased him and sometimes caught him. It seemed to establish a pattern, giving me a victorious feeling to balance the dull night-clerk work.

I became quieter and bolder with my rounds in the dark alleys. I sneaked around until I saw a peeping Tom. The alley was open at both ends, so I threw a rock over the Tom's head to make a noise on the far side. According to the plan, he would turn away from the sound, come toward me, see me, and run, and then I'd catch him.

All was going as planned one night with a particular Tom until he turned toward me. The Tom's silhouette showed a little fellow wearing a scruffy overcoat 30 feet away. I braced myself against the hotel wall, ready to pounce when he came close.

But he didn't play the game. When he saw me, he didn't turn and run. Instead, he stopped, put one hand into his overcoat pocket, and then slowly walked by. I just stood against the hotel wall—not moving a muscle.

I quickly assessed the experience and reverted back to my noisy round procedures. I decided that was enough for my $2.50-per-week's salary.

After a long dry spell, the Oklahoma Dust Bowl in 1933 was roaring across the plains, blowing endless dust in continuous storms. The entire world seemed to be moving around in the atmosphere. Dust was in everything, and everything tasted like Oklahoma. People didn't live on Oklahoma land, they lived *in* it. Having a night job, I used blankets to cover up my windows to blank out the daylight so I could sleep when not in classes. The blankets filled with dirt.

People were leaving Oklahoma for California in droves to find work and escape the dust storms. I considered it, once again dreaming of homesteading Alaska. But I had a college plan going and dream of playing pro-baseball.

Hotel night clerk's pay of $2.50 per week wasn't enough to have fun on. Sandlot baseball was a big sport in Oklahoma City, so I quickly established myself as a winning pitcher for the Biltmore Hotel baseball team, hoping to pitch my way into a job, which I did.

I ran the night elevator at the upscale Biltmore that was 24-stories high. I learned how to scotch my knees and sleep standing up. It was a skill I never used later in life. At an hourly rate of 15 cents (later 22 cents), I became financially independent, allowing me to pay off the $35 tab I had run up with John. I bought a used Ford Model A Coupe for $150—a great joy. John also drove it. Nobody needed driver's licenses in those days.

Only Once a Hobo. I hitchhiked the Oklahoma-Tennessee route home and back several times, always in the summer. (I couldn't afford to drive it.) During good weather, I'd sleep in graveyards or, in rainy weather, in courthouses. Public buildings with benches in them seldom were locked. On one unforgettable occasion in the boondocks of eastern Oklahoma, the weather was poorly, and hitchhiking travel had slowed down, so I decided not to risk being stranded for the night. I joined several hobos at a nearby station who were unloading a freight train headed east. I climbed aboard when the train moved out.

It was a local, slow train through Oklahoma and Arkansas, stopping at all the stations. The brakeman beat on the sides and yelled for help whenever loading or unloading was necessary. More than a dozen of us hobos provided labor, and the trip was fairly pleasant, but dirty. The air was full of coal cinders.

The group was friendly, mostly young farm hands, but it was not a social gathering. We sat on the box car floor and stared at the rocking walls, wishing for a better way to travel. I learned we would get to Little Rock before midnight and to leave the train before it entered the train yard. Train yards were not for hobos. They had railroad detectives who were hostile toward them.

So when the train slowed coming into Little Rock, I de-trained. I walked around to the east side of the station to catch a fast freight to Memphis. I was too filthy to qualify for any other means of transportation. On my way, I stopped at a small all-night cafe where they verified the track location and time of the Memphis train and even gave me an engine number to identify it. Depression-era hoboing had some semblance of order.

That Memphis train had 30 or 40 hobos hanging on ladders and railings and occupying full open-top cars. (Empty, open-top box cars that had been so handy on the local train were rare.) We stopped a few times on traffic control sidings and to pick up water. The brakeman packed a gun and threw rocks at us. At each stop, discreet shuffling occurred among the hobos avoiding the brakeman and seeking better accommodations on the train.

Approaching Memphis, I was in an open-top car empty of its coal as part of the dirtiest, roughest looking group to enter Tennessee. I partnered up with a big, gawky country boy looking as out of place as I felt, and we spent the last few hours going into Memphis sitting back-to-back to provide what turned out to be unnecessary security. After we crossed the Mississippi River, the train slowed a bit, so I left and watched it disappear toward the yards. I promised myself I'd never be a hobo again—and I kept that promise.

Dawn found a half-dozen of us hobos bathing in the river beneath the railroad bridge. It was a futile effort without soap. To implement Hitchhiking Technique Number One, I turned my shirt inside-out, trying to look cleaner. Then, I got a shave, falling asleep in the barber's chair. None of that helped; I had to use my reserve funds carried in my shoe to buy a bus ticket to Waverly. I spent my time in Waverly resting up from the trip home.

Uncle Major and His Military Action Plan (for Me). Then came the summer of 1935. I already had spent four years in college and wasn't finished. Uncle Major, who was also my longtime fishing partner, invited me to his station at Fort McClellan, Alabama, to fish. He had a history of proselyting for the military among his nephews, and he kept at it that summer.

I slept all morning, and we fished in the afternoon. I was impressed with the lifestyle my bachelor-uncle enjoyed: big set of quarters, full-time maid and cook, a "Striker" to shine his brass and polish his leather, and an attentive sergeant to make sure he got to the places he was supposed to go.

Then one morning that sergeant woke me up and led me off to the post medical office. It seems a CMTC camp like the one I went to at Fort Oglethorpe four years earlier was starting up at Fort McClellan, and you had to have a medical exam to enter. (I was due back at my night elevator job in less than a week.)

The Major advised me that I didn't have to go to the camp but that I could get a good medical exam for free, and heckled me, saying, "You probably couldn't pass an Army physical anyway." I did pass the exam, and a month at Fort McClellan sounded pleasant. But I needed the money from my elevator job to support my last year of college. Uncle Major guaranteed finances for college, and that same afternoon, I moved into camp.

Because of my record of military training (two years of ROTC at the University of Tennessee, including band, and one previous CMTC) and my extensive education (four years of college, no degree), I stood out in the crowd of high-school dropouts. I enrolled as a fourth-year "Blue Course" trainee and became commander of one of the camp units. It was fun.

After camp, I wrote Army Headquarters, advising them of my advanced status in one of their military programs, and requested a commission in the US Army Reserve. We corresponded back and forth, which included my returning several forms and undergoing another physical. On November 23, 1935, I was commissioned a second lieutenant in the Infantry, US Army Reserve—no active duty job, no pay, and no plan for a military job for which I might receive pay in the foreseeable future.

But I didn't get fired from my elevator job when I reported back to Oklahoma City after camp. The hotel was sponsoring a sandlot baseball team that summer and still needed a good left-handed pitcher.

By the spring of 1936, I was a winning South Paw pitcher for the OCU Goldbugs. In the three years I had pitched for OCU, I had won two state championships and, playing at the top of the league, claimed squatter's rights to a third. Our last game with Oklahoma University would give us three state championships in a row. It was to be the final event, propelling me into professional baseball.

I was embarrassed at that last game by what happened to my pitches. My team chased me into the showers after the second inning started. Oklahoma University won going away, and no baseball talent scout came forward to claim my services.

I graduated May 29, 1936 from OCU with a Bachelor of Arts degree. I had no plan for the future: pro-baseball was unlikely, and I didn't have the grades for medical school to appease Mother. But Uncle Major had another plan for me: join the US Army. (See Chapter 1 to read about my training as a fighter pilot in the Army Air Corps and first assignment at Langley Field, Virginia.)

Annex III - Graduates in Pursuit Aviation
A Company, Advanced Flying School
Kelly Field, Texas, Class of 1938C

The following are the flight students, lieutenants or cadets (Cdts), who graduated from the Advanced Flying School with me in A Company on October 5, 1938 and our section instructors and administrators. As noted, 11 of the 68 students in my section (16%) were promoted to general officers in World War II or by the time they retired from the Air Force.

Section Chief - Capt. Burton Murdock Hovey Jr. (MajGen.)
Operations Officer - Lt. Marvin F. Stalder
Communications Officer – Lt. J. H. Bundy

A Flight
Instructor Lt. Daniel Stone Campbell (MajGen.)
Lt. Gale Eugene Ellis
Lt. William Joseph Cain Jr.
Lt. William Ray Clingerman Jr.
Lt. John Gordon Eriksen
Lt. Richard William Fellows

B Flight
Instructor Lt. Benjamin Jepson Webster (LtGen.)
Lt. Harry Edwin Hammond
Lt. Thomas Alexander Holdiman
Lt. Bruce Keener Holloway (Fighter Ace, Gen.)
Lt. Richard Phillip Klocko (LtGen.)

C Flight
Instructor Lt. Edwin S. Chickering (BrigGen.)
Cdt. Harry J. Bullis
Cdt. William Hubbert Cleveland

Cdt. Francis Robert Feeney
Cdt. Willard Asa Fountain
Cdt. Philip Henry Greasley (BrigGen.)

D Flight
Instructor Lt. Roy W. Osborn
Cdt. Arnold Frederick Adolph Kluever
Cdt. John Patrick Healy
Cdt. Glenn Elwood Hubbard
Cdt. Elton Earle Holcomb
Cdt. John Max Knox

E Flight
Instructor Lt. Jesse W. Campbell
Cdt. Joe Lennard Mason
Cdt. Frank E. O'Brien
Cdt. Robert Ross McKenchie
Cdt. William Elza McEntire
Cdt. John William Osborn

F Flight
Instructor Lt. Robert Francis Worden (MajGen.)
Cdt. Willian Jesse Prichard
Cdt. John Alva Roberts Jr.
Cdt. Robert Sidney Quinn
Cdt. Gladywyn Earl Pinkston (BrigGen.)

H Flight
Instructor Lt. Dyke F. Meyers
Lt. John Dudley Stevenson (MajGen.)
Lt. John Russell Ulricson
Lt. Charles William Stark Jr.
Lt. Harold Bell Wright
Cdt. Forrest Houston Baxter

I Flight
Instructor Lt. Nelson P. Jackson
Lt. Morton David Magoffin
Lt. Charles Andrew Sprague
Lt. Charles Louis Robbins
Lt. Ivan Wilson McElroy (BrigGen.)
Lt. Charles John Bondley Jr. (MajGen.)

J Flight
Instructor Lt. William Eades
Cdt. Raymond Paul Salzarulo
Cdt. Eriksen Emerson Shilling
Cdt. Paul Schwartz
Cdt. Walter William Sparks Jr.
Cdt. Van Hatton Slayden

K Flight
Instructor Lt. F.N. Ward
Cdt. LeRoy Len Stefonowicz
Cdt. William Alexander Sullivan Jr.
Cdt. James Fred Starkey
Cdt. Ozburn Early Taylor
Cdt. Wayne Earl Thurman

L Flight
Instructor Lt. Chester L. Sluder
Cdt. Joseph Charles Tuell
Cdt. Brewster Ward
Cdt. Raymond Frederick Toliver
Cdt. Sam Wilkins Westbrook III
Cdt. Arthur James Walker

M Flight
Instructor Lt. J.K. Guilmartin
Cdt. Samuel Bey Wiper
Cdt. Ira Francis Wintermute
Cdt. Paul John Yurkanis
Cdt. Guy Hamilton Rockey

Sources: Composite photograph of A Company, class of 1938C, and the graduation program, "Class of October 5, 1938, Air Corps Training Center, Kelly Field, Texas."

For more information about the general officers listed, see www.af.mil/about-us/biographies.

Annex IV – The Making of World War II Warriors: Fighter Pilots in the 24th Pursuit Squadron, 16th Pursuit Group, Albrook Field, Panama

This annex lists the 26 fighter pilots who flew down to Panama with me through Central America in 1939 on orders to report to the 24th Pursuit Squadron to defend the Canal Zone plus other pilots I knew in the squadron or our parent 16th Pursuit Group (Interceptor) during my 1939 – 1941 tour at Albrook Field. Together, we devised the air operations, tactics, techniques, procedures, and training to defend Panama in P-36A Hawks and, then in 1941, in P-40N Warhawks.

At junior ranks we became squadron commanders to fill out the 16th and 32nd Pursuit Groups in Panama. Little did we realize that our experiences would prepare a large number of us to command fighter groups, wings, and higher units in just a couple of years in World War II. Unfortunately, a few pilots in our rudimentary early fighter operations would not live to deploy to World War II. But of those who did, a remarkable number were promoted to general officers, as noted. The 24th Pursuit Squadron—with the insignia of a "Leaping Tiger"—developed Army Air Forces' (AAF's) warriors and leaders for World War II.

1. We 26 lieutenants were to fly fighter aircraft (mostly P-36's) down to Albrook Field on the Pacific Ocean side of Panama. We were notified by "Special Orders No. 201, War Department, Washington DC, 29 August 1939," flying from Barksdale Field, Louisiana; Langley Field, Virginia; and Selfridge Field, Michigan.

We were ordered to fly "via the best available route to the San Antonio Air Depot, Duncan Field, San Antonio, Texas, where personnel and airplanes will be organized into flights....Each officer will then proceed, by order of the Secretary of War, via military aircraft...to Brownsville, Texas, thence to

Tampico, Mexico; Terjeria (Vera Cruz), Mexico; Minatitlin, Mexico; San Geronimo, Mexico; Tapachula, Mexico; Guatemala City, Guatemala; San Salvador, El Salvador; Managua, Nicaragua; San Jose, Costa Rica; David, Republic of Panama; thence to Albrook Field, Canal Zone." We lost two airplanes and one pilot on our trip down Central America.

Barksdale Field
Herman Billings
John Adolph Herman Miller
William Emmett Stinson
Clarence Leonard (Bud) Tinker Jr.

Langley Field
Paul Montgomery Brewer Jr.
John Bailey Henry Jr. (MajGen.)
J. Garrett Jackson
James (Jim) Daniel Mayden
Robert Burl Mueller
Philip Orville Potter
Kyle Loyd Riddle (BrigGen.)
Van Hatton Slayden

Selfridge Field
James Alex Barnett
Robert (Bob) Lee Baseler
Eugene Louis Clark
McDonald H. Hays
Harry Albert Jenkins
Archibald (Archie) Woodrum Moore
Ralph Llewelyn Pusey
George Frederick Ranney
Robert R. (R.R.) Rowland (Fighter Ace, MajGen.)
Burton Eugene Schwind
Joseph Columbus Smith
William Howard Swanson
*John Russell Ulricson
Clinton (Clint) C. Wasem

2. Other pilot friends (I can remember)—cohorts and bosses.
Frank M. Andrews (LtGen.)
Edwin Bishop Jr.
Roger James Browne (MajGen.)
Arthur R. Bump
Edward Cate

Lewis W. Chick Jr.
Thomas Connell Darcy (MajGen.)
Herbert Arthur Dargue (MajGen.)
Adlai H. Gilkeson (BrigGen.)
John Kenton Hester (MajGen.)
Richard T. King (BrigGen.)
James K. Johnson
Philip B. Klein
Sam Maddux Jr. (LtGen.)
George H. MacIntyre
Von R. Shores (MajGen.)
*Marvin F. Stalder
Otto Paul Weyland (Gen.)

*Also in my section at the Advanced Flying School, Kelly Field, Texas, that graduated October 5, 1938.

For more information about these general officers, see www.af.mil/about-us/biographies.

Annex V – Side Story: I am Coronado's Child, Searching for the Lost Dutchman's Goldmine

In late 1942 at Luke Field, Arizona, in the spare time produced by one less workday, I began looking for gold in the Arizona desert. Lieutenant William W. Roberts, one of my flying instructors, brought me a map his uncle had to the legendary Lost Dutchman's Goldmine in the nearby Superstition Mountains.

It really wasn't a map, per se, but a tracing of his uncle's map with a translation of the instructions for it. Mr. H.V. Kruse, the uncle, was an Assistant Engineer for Phelps Dodge Corporation out of Douglas, Arizona.

I talked to Mr. Kruse at length. The map was handed down and the result of "range talk," the source of all information on the Lost Dutchman Goldmine. We agreed that if I found the gold, I would split it with him 50-50.

The story of the map goes like this. Just prior to the beginning of 1845, a young man living on the Peralta Ranch in Mexico committed a crime for which he could be shot. He lit out for Arizona, which at that time was part of Mexico. The ranch owner sent two Indians after him. They caught him in the Superstition Mountains just outside of Phoenix and found him working a rich outcropping of gold ore. The three loaded their horses with almost pure gold and started south back toward the ranch.

Apaches saw what they were doing and set out after them. When the ranch Indians and young man arrived at the Gila River, it was flooded, but they had to risk crossing it or be captured or killed by the Apaches. Only one of the Indians made it back to the ranch, but he was loaded with his portion of the gold.

The Peraltas organized an expedition to get more of the gold and were successful—up to a point. There was much more gold than they could carry on the few horses they had brought. As the story goes, they hid the excess gold near the mine.

As soon as they returned to the ranch, the Peraltas organized a much larger expedition and started north. But this time, the Apaches were ready for them, killing most of the party before it reached the mine.

Arizona became part of the United States in 1845, which, along with the Apache attacks, might have accounted for why the Peralta family never made another attempt to get the gold from the cache or work the mine.

In 1885, a prospector named Jacob Walz, known as the "Dutchman," began showing up in Phoenix with a high grade of gold ore. He went into the Superstition Mountains and came out with quality gold many times before he died in about 1903. On his death bed, the Dutchman told how he had gotten the mine. Jacob said he was crossing the mountains from the north on his way to Florence and found three Mexicans working a rich outcropping. He caught the three unaware and shot them.

While working the mine, he was followed several times and admitted killing seven more people to keep the location of his mine a secret. Evidence indicated there was high-grade gold ore somewhere in the Superstitions. Legend had it that Jacob's mine was somewhere around Weaver's Needle. The Dutchman may have taken out most of the gold, but chances are there was still some left.

The map I got from Mr. Kruse fit into the story as follows. The man who had the map was a cowboy at Fort McDowell. Sometime in the 1880's, he kept company with an Indian girl, an orphan who lived with her grandfather. One day, the cowboy hired out to go to New Mexico to bring back a herd of cattle. Before he left, the grandfather asked him if he was serious about the girl. The cowboy said he was and intended to marry her after he got back from New Mexico when he had money. The grandfather told him that if he only wanted money to marry her, the grandfather could show him where to get plenty of gold.

He told the cowboy that, a few years back, three Mexicans had gone into the Superstition Mountains and started taking out gold. The Apaches followed them and found a white man had joined them at the mine. When the Apaches approached, the Mexicans began shooting, so the Apaches killed them. The white man ran off, and the Apaches didn't bother him.

After the grandfather told him the story, he gave the cowboy a map and letter describing where the map started, which were taken off one of the slain Mexicans. The cowboy refused to give up his trip to New Mexico to go look for the mine, and when he returned, he heard stories about the Dutchman killing people who went into the mountains. The cowboy gave up the idea of looking for the mine.

When the Dutchman died, the cowboy tried to find the mine. He had the map but, by this time he had lost the letter explaining the map's starting point. The map was a rough sketch of several mountains and a large canyon with several smaller canyons (water courses) branching off. One of the smaller canyons clearly had a hole in a side cliff. The Spanish instructions on the map said go up the small canyon until you can see blue sky over your left shoulder through a hole in the cliff. Then locate a mesquite stump on the left slope (going up the canyon). Twenty paces north of this stump in the bottom of the canyon is the mine.

The cowboy scoured the country around Weaver's Needle off and on for 30 years and even had a group of Chinamen looking for the mine with him. When he got too old to prospect for the mine, he gave the map to a Mexican miner friend who had been grubstaking him. The Mexican brought the map to Mr. Kruse, a friend of his, when the Mexican became too old to prospect. Mr. Kruse was interested in the map because it was made of a finely woven cloth covered with petroleum wax, a map that was obviously old.

Sometime later, through a friend who worked on Roosevelt Dam, Mr. Kruse got a copy of the topographical map of the Superstitions made when the dam was being built. Completed in 1903, the dam was just north of the Superstitions. In survey work to establish the water shed of the dam, the government prepared a reasonably accurate contour map of the entire Superstitions area.

Mr. Kruse scaled down his goldmine map, used it like an overlay on the contour map, and sized, shifted, and reoriented the two until they matched. The area was four and one-half miles east of Weaver's Needle going north-northeast up La Barge Canyon Box on an arroyo (wet weather water course) that branched off to the left at the head of the box. So the prospectors had been looking in the wrong place all those years.

A geologist by training, Mr. Kruse's next determined if there was a geological possibility of a mine's being at that place on the map. He found there was. He made a trip into the area, taking with him a Mexican whose ancestors had lived on the Peralta Ranch at the time the family made the gold mining expeditions into the Superstitions. The Mexican gave Mr. Kruse information that indicated his search area was the right one.

Mr. Kruse made four trips into the incredibly harsh Superstition Mountains, and because of a lack of water, which is only available in the winter and in very limited quantities, his partner's breaking his foot, and other difficulties, he never spent more than a few hours searching the area where he thought the Dutchman's goldmine was.

Mr. Kruse never found the gold. But it's notable that neither he nor his Mexican friend paid money for the map. There's no record of the map's ever having been sold. The cowboy, Mexican miner, and Mr. Kruse each, in turn, passed the map on when commonsense told him the Superstitions aren't for old folks.

During the winter of 1942-1943 while stationed at Luke Airfield, I made three trips into the Superstition Mountains looking for the Lost Dutchman's Goldmine, each in the 24 hours of my day off. I went with two officers, Lieutenant William Roberts, Mr. Kruse's nephew-in-law, and Major Quinten Corley, a colleague of mine—partners who were up for an adventure. We each would get one-third of my 50 percent split with Mr. Kruse

We started at midnight on Saturday and drove 60 miles to the road's end in the mountains. That put us in position to tackle the rough stuff at first daylight. We had to make it back to the car on Sunday before darkness set in, meaning that after the hike in, we only had about two hours in the search area. We then drove back to Luke Field in time to start the Monday workday. The expeditions were grueling.

In the first trip, we climbed the wrong mountain, came nowhere near where we should have been, and nearly died of thirst—unaware of how dry the Superstitions were during the winter "wet season." In the second trip, we were well on our way to the right area when we got lost in a dense, winding, fairly tall growth of cactus plants that limited our vision. By the time we figured out where we were, we had to return to the car, knowing we were about right but not far enough up La Barge Canyon. In the third trip, we went to the target area and found a canyon that fit most of the map's description...but not all. Then my two partners went off to war, and my goldmining expeditions ended. Although our trips were unsuccessful, we learned we were children of Coronado.

One summer evening at a Luke Field social event, I met a captain, the new Photographic Officer. He had been issued a K-24 aerial camera and lamented the absence of aircraft on Luke outfitted to support his equipment. A few days later, we flew out to one of the numerous unmanned auxiliary fields supporting Luke's training program. I then tied the camera to the captain's hands and tied him to the AT-6 airplane, more outside than inside. I flew 60 miles to the Superstitions and circled the Dutchman area several times while he snapped away.

Back at the auxiliary field, I untied the frazzled photographic officer who chattered on that he'd never do that again. But a week later, he gave me more than a dozen good aerial pictures of the Superstitions.

I then came down on orders to a unit deploying in World War II. Mr. Kruse requested a report of our searches to add to the saga of his map hanging on his living room wall. So I wrote him about our last expedition and included several aerial pictures of the mountains. Back came his reply with his opinion that we went up the wrong gully. He returned a picture marked "x" where the mine ought to be. Mr. Kruse said we were in the right area, La Barge Canyon Box, but we passed by the wet weather course where the mine was— the course that went off to the left with a cliff running along its left side and a cave-like hole in the cliff showing sky through it. He made a lot of sense, but time had run out. I went off to war.

In June 1944, just before I crossed the English Channel into Normandy, I told the story about the map and my searching for the Lost Dutchman's Goldmine to a group at an officers' club bar. One officer insisted he buy a share in my goldmine and paid me ten dollars for it. I promised him 49 percent of my 1/3 of the 1/2 of the goldmine. But the next day when we were both sober, I returned his ten dollars out of guilt for taking it.

But I was not done yet. At 64 year's old, I went back into the Superstitions in March 1977 with seven members of my family to find the Lost Dutchman's Goldmine. They included my four children and a couple of their spouses: Caroline Weeks, Patty Hollis with husband Jim, and sons Phil Slayden with wife Mary Lynn and Russ Slayden, plus my brother-in-law Jerry Ellis, a retired Air Force lieutenant colonel. They needed a bona fide adventure.

We drove a camper to our home base, Quarter Circle Ranch inside the foothills of the Superstition Mountains near Apache Junction, Arizona. The ranch was six miles away from our target area in the mountains. We hired two guides to get us to the La Barge Canyon, horses to ride, and pack animals for our water and supplies.

The inhospitable Superstition Mountains had rare peculiar "loners" living among them who monitored comings and goings in the mountains. Our guides advised us to strap on handguns before we left the ranch to protect ourselves from rattlesnakes...or whatever. Most of us did. As it turned out, in the three sunshiny days we searched for the mine, we saw four or five flashes of sunlight bouncing off glass in the distance, probably binoculars.

On March 3, we rode the horses with the guides to within a mile of where the map said we'd find the goldmine. The guides left, taking our riding horses, and we hand-walked the pack horses through the particularly narrow and rugged part of the trail. We made camp, spent the night, and got up early for the next three mornings to search the area.

When we made camp that first evening, we scratched the rocky ground, trying to push the biggest rocks aside to lay down our bedrolls; we had to watch out for the many scorpions. There were more rocks than dirt in that ground, so we never got much sleep—mostly just "Rock Therapy," as I renamed it.

For three days, we dug, shoveled and chiseled like miners, sweating in the hot sun. The only water not carried in by us were three small pools that popped up in random places in the otherwise narrow, dry creek bed. We shared that sparse water with a coyote and two wild cows who didn't care if we also were at the pools. We boiled the water from upstream to cook and drink and used the pool downstream to wash (sort of) and water the horses. It was amazing how delicious water, still warm from being boiled, tasted on a hot day, even with a few miscellaneous tidbits floating in it.

One of the days, Patty found a large outcropping of a line of quartz that surfaced off and on across our search area. Quartz, an igneous rock like gold, often accompanies outcroppings of gold. My sons Phil and Russ found a gully that veered to the left of La Barge Canyon Box with an area much smaller than our base camp search area that also seemed to fit the map's description.

The fourth morning, March 7, we broke camp, walked the pack animals out to meet the guides, and rode our horses back to the ranch before nightfall.

We were exhausted, had dust in every pore of our bodies, and hadn't found any gold.

As part of our expedition, I filed a "Notice of Mining Location, Lode Claim," dated March 11 at the Pinal County Recorder's office in Florence, Arizona, for our expedition. I paid four dollars for the claim and named it "Pat's Fault, Nbr One." (We had marked our quartz outcropping claim with a three-and-one-half foot pile of rocks.)

On that March 1977 trip, I fed my and my family's sense of adventure, doing my best to make them Coronado's children.

I'm sure the Lost Dutchman's Goldmine is east of Weaver's Needle in an arroyo that branches off to the left at the top of La Barge Canyon Box and runs north along a fault with vertical cliffs on the arroyo's left side, cliffs that have a cave-like hole through which you can see sky. The mine is below the cave in the bottom of the arroyo 30 to 50 paces north.

There's no doubt in my mind that in at least one of my trips into the Superstition Mountains, I walked right by it.

Annex VI – Checklist for Individual Replacements for Overseas Movement, 27 January 1944

WALTERBORO ARMY AIRFIELD
Office of the Commanding Officer   F-mjh
400.1912   Walterboro, S.C.
27 January 1944.

SUBJECT: Checklist for Individual Replacements for Overseas Movement.

TO : All Base Officers, Walterboro Army Airfield, Walterboro, S. C.

1. The following has been prepared as a checklist for officers in order that necessary preparations may be made for possible overseas assignments:

a. Suggested List of Officers' Clothing and Equipment.

1 Belt, cloth
1 Blouse, woolen
1 Trousers (pink-optional)
2 Trousers (wool –OD)
6 Undershirts (cotton)
6 Drawers (cotton)
24 Handkerchiefs
 3 Undershirts (wool)
3 Drawers (wool)
1 Field Jacket

2 Pajamas (pairs)
 3 Shirts (cotton-khaki)
1 Slippers (pair)
6 Socks (woolen, pairs)
6 Socks (cotton, pairs)
 3 Neckties
2 Garrison Caps (cotton)
2 Leggings (pairs)
1 Bathrobe
 4 Pr. Each, Insignia
1 Shoes (low pair)
2 Shoes (service pairs)
3 Shirts (wool-OD)
1 Overcoat
1 Gloves (pair)
1 Memo Book
1 Each, Fountain Pen and Pencil
1 Brush (shoe)
1 Overshoes (arctic, pair)
1 Raincoat-Trench Coat
1 Muffler (wool)
1 Set Cleaning Materials (brass and shoe)
1 Knife (pocket)
1 Lighter
1 Can Lighter Fluid
1 Razor and 6 Pkgs. Blades
2 Towels (bath-OD)
6 Bars Soap
2 Rolls Toilet Paper
6 Pairs Shoe Lacings
Extra Books (Dict., Bible, etc.)
1 Carton Matches, safety
1 Sunglasses (pair)
1 Watch
2 Toilet Kits
1 Alarm Clock
Above clothing and equipment must be purchased.

b. Items of Issue.

The following items of Quartermaster Equipment may be obtained through issue on shipping ticket to the individual officer:

1 Roll, Bedding, waterproof
2 Blankets, Wool, OD M-34
1 Bag, Canvas, Field
1 Belt, Pistol, Rev M-12 Webb
1 Can, Meat, M-1910
1 Canteen, M-1910
1 Cup, Canteen, Alum. M-1910
1 Cover, Canteen, M/D M-10
1 Fork, M-1910
1 Knife, M-1910
10 Pins, Tent, Shelter
1 Pocket, Magazine
2 Poles, Tent, Shelter
1 Pouch, First Aid
1 Spoon, M-1926
1 Strap, Bag, Canvas
1 Suspenders, Belt, M-36
2 Tent, Shelter, Half
2 Covers, Mattress, Cot
1 Helmet, Steel, M-1
1 Liner, Helmet, M-1
1 Band, Neck, M-1
1 Band, Head, M-1, size ___
1 Locker, trunk **
1 Bag, duffle**
1 Packet, First Aid (Medical Supply)

**Issued only after receipt of orders.

c. Personnel Records.

The following personnel records will be carried on the officer's person upon transfer to a Replacement Depot or Port of Embarkation:

Pay Data Card, WD AGO Form 77
Identification Tags (2) worn around the neck.
WD AGO Form 65-1, Identification Card

WD MD Form 81, Immunization Register
WD AGO Form 66-1 or 66-2, Officer's Classification Card

Copy of orders announcing rating (for flying personnel)
Copy of orders authorizing flying status (for flying personnel)

d. Baggage.

 (1) Baggage will be limited to the following, not to exceed 175
pounds. (An additional 55 pounds of flying clothing and equipment is
authorized in cases of rated flying personnel traveling by water):

One trunk locker when authorized, or barracks bag, if trunk locker
not authorized
One bedding roll, when authorized (not over 50 pounds)
One piece of hand baggage (not over 40 pounds)
One field or musette bag
One A-3 bag for flying equipment (for rated flying personnel)
One duffle bag

 (2) Officers will have only a piece of hand baggage and field or
musette bag in their stateroom. As a general rule, bedding rolls and
trunk lockers will not be accessible during the voyage.

e. Marking of Personnel Baggage.

 All personal baggage (barracks bags, flying bags, trunk lockers, hand
baggage, bedding rolls which accompany individuals to replacement
depot or port of embarkation or are shipped thereto) will be stenciled,
using white (on blue) or black (on white or khaki) lead paste (paint),
with individual's full name (first name, middle initial, and last name),
full serial number, grade, and appropriate shipment number and
letter (if known). Officers' trunk lockers will be marked on both ends.

f. Disposition of Personal Effects.

 Prior to departure from depot or port or from home station to port,
personnel will dispose of all personal effects (superfluous clothing,
collections of personal letters, etc.) which will not be taken overseas.

g. Special Clothing and Equipment.

 Special clothing and equipment as directed in movement orders will be issued at the port of embarkation.

h. Training.

 (1) No individual will be transferred to a personnel depot or port of embarkation for movement overseas unless he has completed the individual training prescribed in Mobilization Training Program or an Army Air Forces Training Standard for his arm or service. His training will include the completion of –
   (a) A qualification course in marksmanship as outlined in the appropriate Field Manual or Mobilization Training Program with any one of the following weapons:

Rifle
Carbine
Pistol (Counterintelligence Corps may fire revolvers)
Submachine gun

(2) Familiarization firing with the type weapon with which he is armed.
   (a) No firing will be required for individuals who will not be armed (chaplains, medical, and WAC personnel).

By order of Colonel PRINCE: GEORGE A. FERGUSON, SR.

                                                Major, Air Corps.
                                                Base Adjutant
                                                SIGNED

Annex VII – Army Indoctrination Training for Redeployment [Humorous], 20 September 1944

I brought this memo back from the WWII European Theater of Operations; a GI wrote it describing mock training required to re-civilize GIs enough to redeploy to the US at the war's end. It was written in September 1944 because, at that point, the Allies were steadily chasing the Nazis back into Germany. The rumor was the war in Europe would be over by Christmas. That was before the Germans pushed back in the Battle of the Bulge in mid-December 1944.

HEADQUARTERS _____ U. S. ARMY
APO 001 U. S. Army

AG 4110.99 AC (DEBGA)   20 September 1944.

SUBJECT: Indoctrination, for return to the U. S.

TO : All Units.

    1. In compliance with current policies for rotation of armed forces overseas, it is directed that, in order to maintain the high standards of character of the American soldier and to prevent any dishonor to reflect on the uniform, all individuals eligible for return to the U.S. under current directives will undergo an indoctrination course of demilitarization prior to approval of his application for return.

    2. The following points will be emphasized in subject indoctrination course:

a. In America there is a remarkable number of beautiful girls. These young girls <u>have not</u> been liberated and many of them are gainfully employed as stenographers, sales girls, beauty operators, or welders. Contrary to current practices, they should not be approached with, "How much?" A proper greeting is, "Isn't it a lovely day?" or "Have you ever been to Chicago?" Then say, "How much?"

b. A guest in a private home is usually awakened in the morning by a light tapping on his door and an invitation to join the host at breakfast. It is proper to say, "I'll be there shortly." DO NOT say, "Blow it out your ____!"

c. A typical American breakfast consists of such strange foods as cantaloupes, fresh eggs, milk, ham, etc. These are highly palatable and though strange in appearance, are extremely tasty. Butter made from cream is often served. If you wish some butter, you turn to the person nearest it and say quietly, "Please pass me the butter." You DO NOT say, "Throw me the goddam grease."

d. Very natural urges are apt to occur when in a crowd. If it is found necessary to defecate, one does not grab a shovel in one hand and paper in the other and run for the garden. At least 90% of American homes have one room called the "Bathroom," i.e., a room that, in most cases, contains a bathtub, wash basin, medicine cabinet, and a toilet. It is the latter that you will use in this case. Instructors should make sure that all personnel understand the operation of a toilet, particularly the lever or button arrangement that serves to prepare the device for re-use.

e. In the event the helmet is retained by the individual, he will refrain from using it as a chair, wash bowl, foot bath, or bathtub. All these devices are furnished in the average American home. It is not considered good practice to squat Indian fashion in the corner in the event all chairs are occupied. The host will usually provide suitable seats.

f. Belching and passing wind in company is strictly frowned upon. If you should forget about it, however, and belch in the presence of others, a proper remark is, "Excuse me." DO NOT say, "It must be that lousy chow we've been getting."

g. American dinners, in most cases, consist of several items, each served in a separate dish. The common practice of mixing various items, such as corn-beef and pudding or lima beans and peaches to make then more palatable will be refrained from. In time the "Separate Dish" system will become enjoyable.

h. Americans have a strange taste for stimulants. The drinks in common usage on the European continent, such as under ripe wine, alcohol and grapefruit juice, or gasoline bitters and water (commonly known by the French term "Cognac") are not ordinarily acceptable in civilian circles. These drinks should be served only to those who are definitely not within the inner circle of friends. A suitable use for such drinks is for serving to one's landlord in order to break an undesirable lease.

i. The returning soldier is apt to often find his opinions differ from those of his civilian associates. One should call upon his reserve of etiquette and correct his acquaintances with such remarks as, "I believe you have made a mistake," or "I'm afraid you are in error in that." DO NOT say, "Brother, you're really F___d UP." This is considered impolite.

j. Upon leaving a friend's home after a visit, one may find his hat misplaced. Frequently it has been placed in a closet. One should turn to one's host and say, "I don't seem to have my hat, could you help me find it?" DO NOT say, "Don't anybody leave this room, some S.O.B. has stolen my hat!"

k. In traveling in the U.S., particularly in a strange city, it is often necessary to spend the night. Hotels are provided for this purpose, and one can get directions to the nearest hotel from almost anyone. Here for a small sum, one can register and be shown to a room where he can sleep for the night. The present practice of entering the nearest house, throwing the occupants into the yard, and taking over the premises will cease.

l. Whiskey, a common American drink, may be offered to the soldier on social occasions. It is considered a reflection on the uniform to snatch the bottle from the hostess and drain the bottle, cork and all. All individuals are cautioned to exercise extreme control in these circumstances.

m. In motion picture theaters, seats are provided. Helmets are not required. It is NOT considered good form to whistle every time a female over 8 and under 80 crosses the screen. If vision is impaired by the person in the seat in front, there are plenty of other seats which can be occupied. DO NOT hit him across the back of the head and say "Move your head Jerk, I can't see a damned thing."

n. It is not proper to go around hitting everyone of draft age in civilian clothes. He might have been released from service for medical reasons; ask for his credentials, and if he can't show any, THEN go ahead and slug him.

o. Upon retiring, one will often find a pair of pajamas laid out on the bed. (Pajamas, it should be explained, are two piece garments which are donned after all clothing has been removed.) The soldier, confronted by these garments, should assume an air of familiarity, and act as though he were used to them. A casual remark such as, "My, what a delicate shade of blue," will usually suffice. Under no circumstances say, "How in the hell do you expect me to sleep in a getup like this?"

p. Natural functions will continue. It may be necessary frequently to urinate. DO NOT walk behind the nearest tree or automobile you find to accomplish this. Toilets (2d above) are provided in all public buildings for this purpose. Signs on some doors will read "LADIES" which literally interpreted means "OFF LIMITS TO ALL TROOPS."

q. Beer is sometimes served in bottles. A cap remover is usually available and it is not good form to open the bottle by use of one's teeth.

r. Air raids and enemy patrols are not encountered in America. Therefore, it is not necessary to wear the helmet in church or at social gatherings or to hold the weapon at ready, loaded, and cocked when talking to civilians in the street.

s. Every American home and all hotels are equipped with bathing facilities. When it is desired to take a bath, it is not considered good form to find the nearest pool or stream, strip down and indulge in a bath. This is particularly true in heavily populated areas.

t. All individuals returning to the U.S. will make every effort to conform to the customs and habits of the regions visited and to make themselves as inconspicuous as possible. Any actions which reflect upon the honor of the uniform will be promptly dealt with.

For the Commanding General:

A. J. BLANK
Colonel, A.G.D.

DISTRIBUTION: "X" Adjutant General
Reproduced Hqs ___ Corps
Distribution "XX"

Annex VIII – Tiptoeing through a Nazi Minefield at Brest and "Task Force Slayden" near St. Vith, Letters by Lieutenant Colonel William Marshall Slayden II

The following two letters from Brother Bill Slayden describe exciting missions as a US Army Intelligence Officer for VIII Corps (1944) during the war in Europe. The information in brackets in the letters was added by Bill in 1994 to clarify information censored for security reasons during the war.

The first letter describes Bill tiptoeing through a Nazi minefield under a flag of truce at the port of Brest in northwest France on September 13, 1944 to ask the Germans to surrender. The letter was written to our parents, (Violetta and Ab Slayden) in Waverly.

Brest, known as "Fortress Brest," with 40,000 fighting men from three Wehrmacht divisions and other elements, was commanded by General der Fallschirmtruppe Hermann-Bernhard Ramcke, a veteran paratrooper of the Afrika Korps. US fighting slowly pushed the Nazis back into Brest, but the general's paratroopers fought stubbornly.

VIII Corps' capture of the main port facilities at Brest was important for the invading Allied forces. The Nazi's had severely damaged the deep water port of Cherbourg on the English Channel, and 37 Allied divisions were to invade mainland Europe, requiring 26,000 tons of supplies every day.

General Ramcke refused to surrender. VIII Corps surrounded Brest and fought door-to-door in intense combat with heavy artillery barrages from both sides. The old city of Brest was razed to the ground with only a few medieval stone fortifications left standing. General Ramcke surrendered Brest on September 19 after rendering the port facilities useless.

Somewhere in France [Brest]
G-2 Section, Headquarters [VIII Corps]
September 16, 1944

Dear Mom and Dad:

Today my military career reached a new milestone—I was decorated by Major General Troy H. Middleton [Commanding General of VIII Corps] in an impressive little ceremony in the field before the assembled officers of this corps headquarters. Bronze Star Medals were awarded to me and two other officers for carrying a message through the enemy's lines from General Middleton to Major General Ramcke, the commander of the German forces who were opposing us [at the German submarine base at Brest], offering the Germans the opportunity to surrender before we blasted them out of their entrenchments and destroyed them.

I volunteered for the mission that took place on September 13, knowing full well some hazard would be involved but having no idea we would encounter the extremely dangerous situation in which we found ourselves before we got through. In order to cross the lines, I carried a flag of truce, and we approached the German positions in a vehicle.

A terrific battle was in progress at the point where we decided to cross, and we could see tracer bullets from enemy weapons flying in all directions. As we proceeded down the road past the last American soldier and in constant fear of hitting a mine in the road, we came to iron rails that blocked further passage by vehicle.

We turned to the right onto a side road, hoping to go around, but this road also was blocked a short distance away. While on the side road, bullets were flying thick and fast all around, and one came so close that it passed through our vehicle between the front and rear seats, entering the car on my side. I shan't attempt to describe my reaction when I looked down and saw the hole it tore in the side of the car and realized how near it came to hitting my knee.

After returning to the main road, I waved the flag of truce, and we dismounted and proceeded on foot toward the Germans firing at us about 200 yards ahead. As we approached these positions, we realized that if they didn't stop firing, we would all be killed, but they finally recognized the flag of truce and held their fire.

Presently I saw a head move in the hedgerow ahead and I made him out to be a German soldier. To complete the final distance between ourselves and the German soldiers, we had to thread out way through a minefield laid out in front of their positions. As the American officer walking in front with the white flag, I carefully stepped forward and the two officers behind me stepped exactly in my tracks—of course, waiting to ensure my steps were successful.

For once the sight of a German soldier, even if he did have a gun sighted on us, was a relief because he motioned us forward hollering, "Achtung," occasionally as we got too close to locations near the hedgerows where mines were placed. I cannot tell you what a strange feeling it was to take visual directions from an arch enemy soldier, peeking out of a foxhole some distance in front of you, who was yelling, "Minen!" But we followed his hand waves and got through the field.

We then were ordered into a concrete bunker and our credentials were examined. Our own artillery hit the bunker, but it was a very strong one and could withstand the heaviest pounding. From this point, we were blindfolded and escorted outside deeper inside the German lines. But then our troubles really started for we were in danger of being hit by our artillery fire, which in several instance, fell so close that the air blast from the explosions knocked us down.

We arrived at another bunker where Colonel Reeves [G-2 of VIII Corps] stated his mission to the major in charge who communicated it to General Ramcke in his headquarters bunker some distance away. Colonel Reeves asked to meet with General Ramcke in person. But the general decided we could not safely travel the distance to his command post blindfolded to deliver the message in the terrific artillery fire and destruction.

We were inside the German lines in the bunker for eight hours and treated very courteously and properly. A Major Hofmann of the German Marines served us cognac and wine as well as very delicious stew, with cigars to follow, and we carried on extensive conversations on nonmilitary subjects through an interpreter by the name of Sergeant Heitman. The sergeant had lived in the Bronx and been in business prior to 1938, marrying an American girl now living in Germany.

Both asked us at different times what prisoners of war were allowed to take with them, and we could see that they realized that either death or capture would be their ultimate fate. A large number of wounded also were crowded into another section of the bunker, and we could hear their moans and groans.

General Ramcke refused to surrender, which if he had, would have saved much blood from being spilt to force the German surrender and capitulation.

Our return trip back across the minefield was not as hazardous as the artillery fire had died down and our men recognized us immediately, so we were not subjected to small arms fire.

I am well and relatively safe now, and, of course, with my medal, my morale is ace high.

All my love,
Bill

This second letter is about Bill's command of "Task Force Slayden" that delayed a large Nazi force in a surprise frontal assault on US forces in the dense Ardennes Forest on the road to St. Vith, Belgium, in the Battle of the Bulge. His actions that day earned Bill an Oak Leaf Cluster to his Bronze Star Medal.

At the time, Bill was the Assistant G-2 of VIII Corps, headquartered at Bastogne; the corps was resting up and retrofitting. The weather was intensely cold, and snow covered the ground.

Bill wrote this letter to our bachelor uncle, Brigadier General George Hatton Weems, our mother's brother, who was then Assistant Commandant of the US Army Infantry School, Fort Benning, Georgia, with the job of training US infantrymen for war. We affectionately and respectfully called him "Uncle General." He was the Patriarch of the "Fighting Weemses."

This letter is about Bill's actions on December 16, 1944, the first day of the Battle of the Bulge.

Somewhere in Belgium [St. Vith]
G-2 Section, Headquarters, [VIII Corps]
January 3, 1945

Dear Uncle General:

You, of course, know by now that you left this part of the country too soon for the big show [Battle of the Bulge]. And as luck (good or bad, I haven't decided yet) would have it, I was right at the point of impact when the blow struck.

The outfit [2d Infantry Division] that you and I visited when you were here had just been relieved by a new unit. The new G-2 was a nervous Nelly, so Colonel Reeves [G-2, VIII Corps] sent me to "hold his hand" while they were getting set in their new positions. I had been with the unit three days, and things were going smoothly—except that "Jerry" had been unusually quiet, and we were wondering what he was up to.

The morning of my fourth day [December 16, 1944], they hit us. During the morning of the first day of the attack, it did not appear to be a big show; but at noon, we captured a complete order for the whole show from Rundstedt [Field Marshall von Rundstedt, German Commander-in-Chief West] down through a new division on our front, and then we knew the extent of this effort.

That afternoon, I tried to get out to the command post where Colonel Hirschfelder had his unit, but by the time I got out there, the left flank of that new unit had crumbled and was in danger of being cut off. By 0900 hours the next day, that unit and the unit to the right were both cut off, and the situation was very confused.

Before I got to the little town where the bridge crosses the river and the road starts up the hill, I ran into the enemy myself. Nothing was between the enemy and the command post [106th Infantry Division at St. Vith] I just left, except several miscellaneous vehicles I had passed and withdrawing artillery. At 1145 hours, I tapped into a line with a field telephone and reported the situation to the CG [Commanding General of the 106th Infantry Division, Major General A.W. Jones]. He instructed me to delay the enemy as long as possible so an engineer battalion [81st] had time to prepare the close-in defense [for St. Vith].

I met up with Lieutenant Colonel Earle Williams, [106th Infantry] division Signal Officer, and Sergeant Clyde Foster, his wire chief, at the division forward switching central [Schonberg on the road to St. Vith]. They were frantically clearing the Allied traffic, preparing to destroy the switchboard.

Now, we two lieutenant colonels began to operate like platoon commanders. Williams and I joined our detachment of men, three Jeeps (each with a .30 caliber machinegun) and an armored car (with a .50-caliber machinegun) into a task force to delay the enemy's advance. Most Belgium roads in the Ardennes had trees along the shoulders; Williams felled these trees across the road to create a block. When the enemy appeared at a block or a turn in the road, we would lay down as much fire as we could and call in artillery fire as well.

This would cause the enemy to stop and deploy infantry soldiers in white camouflage snowsuits around our flanks to discover what the opposition was. When their fire got too heavy or too close, we fell back. Then when the enemy found no opposition (since we had withdrawn to the next curve or road block), the Germans would return to their personnel carriers. Thus we delayed their advance.

For four hours, "Task Force Slayden" put up a big show at each bend in the road until the Germans brought up tanks, and then we had to scram. We almost waited too long a couple of times. We delayed this armored thrust until the Germans pushed us back three miles to where the engineer battalion was taking its defensive positions about a mile east of the division's headquarter. Other forces took over [81st and 168th Engineer battalions with the 592nd Field Artillery Battalion], but that's their story.

In Task Force Slayden, I had never shot at more Germans or been shot at by more Germans in all the war put together. At one climactic moment, I stepped around a bend in the road and suddenly came face-to-face with a German soldier dressed in white, obviously a point man for the Nazi panzers, only to discover that my pistol wouldn't fire. Luck was certainly with me as I beat a hasty retreat under his fire without being scratched.

We held that town [St. Vith] for the next three or four days under terrific shelling, pulled out just in time, and then almost got cut off again before the situation stabilized. It was ten days before I got back to [VIII Corps] Headquarters, which in the meantime had been pushed out of the location where you visited me [Bastogne]. The town itself held out although it's now in shambles. We've all been as busy as birddogs in November—and still in the thick of it.

Love to all your girls,
Bill

P.S. I was with [Major General] A. W. Jones, and he sends his regards.

Sources for this Annex. Letters written by Lieutenant Colonel Bill Slayden reprinted from *Weemsana,* Official Newspaper of the G.H. Weems Educational Fund, Volume XXXX, Number 1, Waverly, Tennessee, dated July 1994, Pages 12-13; Wikipedia, "Battle for Brest" online; "The Battle of the Bulge," a 33-page document by Bill Slayden in 13-segments as articles for 1999-2000 publication in the *Waverly News Democrat*; a daily diary written by Bill Slayden as Assistant G-2 of VIII Corps, Book 1: Thursday, May 11, 1944 to Monday, October 2, 1944, and Book 2: Tuesday, October 3, 1944 to Sunday, January 7, 1945, information that he embellished with details after the war; and "A World War II Experience as told by Col. William M. Slayden II, US Army Retired, The Battle of the Bulge" online at

http://www.grunts.net/wars/20thcentury/wwii/slayden/slayden4.html.

Annex IX – Command & Staff Officers, 36th Fighter Group, April 1945

The following are my command and staff officers (alphabetical order) in the 36th Fighter Group, XIX Tactical Air Command, based at Y-62 Airfield, Koblenz, Germany, as of early April, 1945:

LtCol. Van H. Slayden, CO, 36th Fighter Group
LtCol. Joseph K. Kirkup, Deputy CO, 36th Fighter Group
LtCol. Brendan E. Toolin, Group Executive

Maj. Wilton H. Earle, CO, 22nd Fighter Squadron
Maj. Alfred R. Weegar, CO, 23rd Fighter Squadron
LtCol. John L. Wright, CO, 53rd Fighter Squadron

Anderson, Wm B., 1Lt. - Weather Officer
Audzik, Francis P., 1Lt. - Aerial Photo Interpretation
Bielanico, Jack R., 1Lt. - Fly Control
Brownwell, Harold, Capt. - Group Personnel
Coe, David C., 1Lt. - Air Inspector
Dalton, Jr., Henry H., Capt. - Special Services
Foster, Virgil C., 1Lt. - Aerial Photo Interpretation
Gardner, Rufus H., Capt. - Ground Liaison Officer (GLO)
Gibson, William H., 1Lt. - Planning and Reporting Officer (PRO)
Hart, John W., 1Lt. - Medical Supply
Hayes, Rutherford B., Capt. - Military Police
Hayutin, Harvey E., 1Lt. - Group Supply
Hermes, Richard L., Maj. - Surgeon
Holmes, Chas. H., Capt. - Examination & Inventory (Maintenance)
Horst, Urban J., W/O - Tech Inspector
Jackson, Benjamin H., Capt. - Amory & Ordinance
Jones, Thomas K., Capt. - Dental Surgeon

LaRoque, Richard W., Maj. - Operations Officer
McMurray, James E., Capt. - Arm & Chem
Messmer, William J., Maj. - Communications Officer
Peacock, James E., Capt. - Intelligence Officer
Phelps, Ralph E., 1Lt. - Asst. Communications
Phelps, Richard N., Capt. - Asst. Operations
Presslar, Oscar, 1Lt. - Fly Control
Read, Jr., Charles D., 1Lt. - Asst. Intelligence
Right, David P., 1Lt. - Fly Control
Smith, James A., Maj. - Supply and Evacuation Officer
Saunders, Louis A., Capt. - Chaplain
Thaler, Daniel A., 1Lt. - Radar Officer
Todd, Lawrence E., 1Lt. - Engineering
Van Stuck, William, Capt. - Intelligence
Walker, Jr., Walter B., Capt. - Air Inspector
Wessels, Delano E., Capt. - Tech Inspector
Whipple, Dodge L., Maj. - Group Adjutant
Williams, Jr., Robert T., 1Lt. - Stat Control

Sources for this Book

The late Van Slayden's revisions of four drafts of his memoirs and information gleaned from his official military records and certificates of training, graduation, and achievements; official 36th Fighter Group monthly data/operations reports during his command; historical accounts of the times, and 1920 - 1940 Census of Waverly, Tennessee; more than 100 family letters, family genealogy papers, Bible records, family memorabilia, and firsthand accounts; official 1938, '39 and '40 US Army Air Corps Accident Reports (Aviation Archaeology Investigation & Research); and for the friendly fire incident, official 36th Fighter Group March 1945 unit report, carbon copies of the statements by the P-47 and P-51 pilots and 36th Fighter Group staff, the IX Tactical Air Command (TAC) mission order, P-51 Missing Air Crew Report (MACR), the Mosquito's 25th Bombardment Group (Reconnaissance) March 1945 unit report, and P-51's 435th Fighter Squadron's (479th Fighter Group) March 1945 unit report. Historical documents include five original *The Stars and Stripes* newspapers for the European Theater reporting various significant events in 1944 and 1945, and research on Wikipedia, Britannica, Inc., The National Archives' *Air Force Combat Units of World War II,* Parts 1 – 8 (Maurer, Maurer), *Army Air Forces in World War II* (7 Volumes) by Wesley Frank Craven and James Lea Cate, under the auspices of the Office of Air Force History, printed by the University of Chicago Press, January 1, 1983; and other Army Air Corps and US Air Force reports, publications, and photographs. A booklet "Once Upon a Time" of 8 x 10-inch cartoons drawn by Van Slayden of his tours in the USAAC and then USAF, from Advanced Flight School at Kelly Field, Texas, in 1938 to his retirement in Waverly, Tennessee, in 1962; in the cartoons he writes the names of people he and, later, his wife Caroline knew and worked with at each station. Additional sources are noted in the body of the book for immediate credibility and referenced at the end of annexes.

Patrecia Slayden Hollis

Acknowledgements

First, I give special thanks to my sister Caroline Weems (Slayden) Weeks, and brother Russell Cameron Slayden who supported me throughout this project and the wonderful Slayden Brothers cousins: the late Alvin Weems (Skipper) Slayden Jr. and Billie Carolyn (Slayden) Gnodde (Al Slayden Family) and Dr. Suzanne Weems Slayden and William Marshall Slayden III (Bill Slayden Family) for their help with family information, research and finding photographs—but mostly for their enthusiasm. I would be remiss if I didn't single out Ruth Slayden, Skipper's widow, who is one of my cheerleaders for this project and an internet research wiz and her stepdaughter Cheryl (Slayden) Michalowski, who guarded a stash of World War II family letters for years and shared them with gusto, bringing both greater detail and depth to Dad's memoirs. I must thank my grandmother, the late Violetta Chapman (Weems) Slayden, for keeping every scrap of paper related to her sons, right down to Dad's elementary school grade cards, and for training Dad to do the same. I thank Jonathan Bernard, the Director of the US Army Air Defense Artillery Museum on Fort Sill, Oklahoma, and an author working on his third book on P-47 Thunderbolt fighter-bomber units in all World War II theaters for his invaluable assistance. He reviewed my early manuscript, provided additional historical data and insights into P-47 pilot operations during the war, and shared photos relevant to these memoirs. Last, but certainly not least, I thank Captain James Taylor, USN retired, a submariner who worked with Tom Clancy on technically reviewing the *Hunt for Red October,* marketing the book, and serving as technical expert for the crew filming the book; James gave me feedback on the book and advice on marketing it. Thank you all for helping me publish Van Slayden's firsthand account of air operations in World War II in the European Theater and contributing to the US Air Force's early fighter history.

Patrecia Slayden Hollis

Glossary

AAC = Army Air Corps

AAF = Army Air Forces

AF = Air Force

AWOL = away without leave

Bandits = enemy aircraft

Bogies = unidentified aircraft

CAS = close air support

CO = commanding officer

ETO = European Theater of Operations

GI = member of the US Armed Forces, also an acronym for "Government Issue"

GP = general purpose (bomb)

GUMP = acronym for air operations checklist: Gas (on the correct tank), Undercarriage (in the correct position), Mixture (of fuel for the job at hand), and Propeller (at the right pitch)

HQ = Headquarters

KIA = killed in action

Le Boche = French slur for Germans, meaning, in polite terms, thickheaded, disagreeable, and troublesome

MACR = Missing Air Crew Report

ME = maximum effects

MIA = missing in action

MP = Military Police

Nazi = National Socialist German Workers' Party (Nationalsozialistishce Deutsche Arbeiterpartei)

OD = olive drab

P/W = prisoner of war

RAF = Royal Air Force
RMS = Royal Majesty's Service
ROTC = Reserve Officers' Training Corps
R/T = radio/teletype
R.T.D. = returned to duty (MACR)
SHAEF = Supreme Headquarters, Allied Expeditionary Forces
TAC = Tactical Air Command
USAAF = US Army Air Forces
USAF = US Air Force
USSAFE = US Strategic Air Forces in Europe
VE = Victory in Europe
VIP = very important person
WAC = Women's Army Corps
WAVES = Women Accepted for Volunteer Emergency Service (US Navy)
W/O = Warrant Officer

Note from the Author

Word-of-mouth is crucial for any author to succeed. If you enjoyed *Normandy to Nazi Surrender*, please leave a review online—anywhere you are able. Even if it's just a sentence or two. You also can go to my website, www.pshollisauthor.com, and share your comments under "Contact" on the website's menu. Or you can email me at Pat@pshollisauthor.com. It would make all the difference and would be very much appreciated.

Thanks!
Patrecia Slayden Hollis

About the Authors

Colonel Phillip Van H. Slayden (1913 – 1996), US Air Force Retired, taught Military History at West Point, served as US Chief Advisor to rehabilitate the Republic of Korea Air Force after the war, and commanded the 4504th Missile Wing at Orlando AFB, Florida, among other assignments. From flying bi-wing aircraft in 1937 to standing up America's first Intercontinental Ballistic Missile (ICBM) School in 1959, Van Slayden advanced the most powerful Air Force in history.

Patrecia Slayden Hollis collaborated with her father on this book. She was Editor of the Army and Marine Corps professional journal, *Field Artillery*, for 20 years at Fort Sill, Oklahoma, interviewing for publication 80-plus combat veterans, including division and corps commanders returning from the Middle East. She received the Dallas Press Club's 1996 Katie Award and Statue for Best Interview with Marine Lieutenant General John F. Sattler, "The Second Battle of Fallujah—Urban Operations in a New Kind of War."

Thank you so much for reading one of our **Non-Fiction** books.

If you enjoyed our book, please check out our recommendation for your next great read!

Battle Hymn by John Scura and Dane Phillips

REVELATIONS OF THE SINISTER PLAN

FOR A NEW WORLD ORDER

Made in United States
Orlando, FL
27 February 2023